Captai

MICK

NAME OF THE GAME – Mick McCarthy gets a header for Manchester City against Brighton's Gerry Ryan (1983/84 season)

Mick McCarthy

To my wife Fiona

and my children Anna, Katie and Michael

CAPTAIN FANTASTIC

My Football Career and World Cup Experience

Mick McCarthy

Researched and Edited by
Matthew Nugent
Colour photographs: The Star

THE O'BRIEN PRESS
DUBLIN

First published 1990 by The O'Brien Press, 20 Victoria Road, Rathgar, Dublin 6, Ireland.

British Library Cataloguing in Publication Data
McCarthy, Mick
Captain Fantastic: my football career & World cup experience.
1. (Republic) Ireland. Association football. McCarthy, Mick
I. Title
796.334092
ISBN 0-86278-237-6

PHOTOGRAPHS
We thank the following:
The Star for colour photographs – photographers
Noel Gavin and Jim Walpole.
Black and White: p.1 *Manchester Evening News*; p.2 Harry Godwin;
p.6 Noel Gavin; pp.10,12 McCarthy family photographs; pp.13,14 Ray
Sabine; p.22 *Barnsley Chronicle*; p.27 *Sunday People*;
p.40 *Glasgow Evening Times*; pp.36, 42, 43 *Scottish Daily Record*

10 9 8 7 6 5 4 3 2

Typeset at The O'Brien Press
Printed by the Guernsey Press Co. Ltd., Guernsey, Channel Islands

Contents

MY FOOTBALL CAREER

EURO '88

THE WORLD CUP 1990

Acknowledgements

Many people have helped me throughout my life, helped mould my character, put me on the straight and narrow or were generally just there to help when they were needed. Others were also good friends! So my thanks go to my parents Charles and Josephine McCarthy for being there when I needed them and for being the best Mother and Father anyone could ask for. To my Gran, Mary Taylor – God bless you. To my sister Catherine and brothers John and Kevin. To my wife Fiona's parents, Pat and Jack Morgan, who have always been there for both of us down through the years.

To all my friends in Barnsley, especially Bols (Jonathan Ansell), my mate Glyn Robinson and his wife Linda, Cush (Robin Caulfield) and Tim Andrews and his wife Sharon. Schoolteachers played a big part in my early life – for many different reasons! So I would like to thank Bob and Hazel Gibbs, Les Foweather, and Ed Gabbani, my old fifth-form teacher. Hello Mick Hayselden and Denbo (Dennis Griffiths), landlord at Worsbrough's finest pub, The Red Lion.

I would also like to express my appreciation to Keith Steele, Lord rest him, who played a huge part in getting my football career off the ground and to his father Johnny who helped me sign for Barnsley, and to Norman Rimmington for all the great advice he gave me when I was at Oakwell.

My former neigbours in Wilmslow, May and Lou Jones, and Mike and Sandra Williams, and my best friend from my Man City days Woody (Mike Woods). Oh, and hello Roland Holloway – thanks for everything.

To the nicest Rangers supporters in the world, Billy Cowan and his wife Alison – thanks for being great neighbours in Scotland. And an especially big thanks to all the Celtic supporters who made my stay at the club so wonderful. *Merci* to Peter and Helena Boyle in Lyons, and the same again to George Halatas, the best physiotherapist I have ever come across.

Cheers to Taffy (Ian Evans) – we had some great times together at Barnsley ... let's do the same thing at Millwall.

A special thank you to Mick Byrne. Without his help and care I might still be on thirty caps! And to all our wonderful supporters ... keep it up. To John Casey, one of many unsung heroes in Irish Junior football; without him the game would never survive. And to all my managers: Jim Iley, Allan Clarke, Norman Hunter, Billy McNeill, Jimmy Frizzell, David Hay, Raymond Domenech, Bob Pearson, Bruce Rioch, Eoin Hand and Jack Charlton … thanks for taking a chance on me, I hope I didn't let you down.

Very special thanks to Matt Nugent, to Geraldine Nugent who spent hours trying to decipher my notes and to Mr and Mrs Thomas Nugent who made me feel at home as we put this book together. And thanks to two people who gave me such courage during the World Cup – my little friend Michael McCarthy and his father.

Mick McCarthy

Mick McCarthy with Matthew Nugent

STARTING OUT WITH BARNSLEY

THE WHOLE OF ITALY – AND IRELAND – CAME TO A STANDSTILL for a few hours on Saturday evening, June 30, 1990. All eyes focused on the Olympic Stadium in Rome as the Republic of Ireland team made their last-minute preparations to take on the Italians in the quarter-finals of the World Cup. For twenty-one days that month all worries and problems had been set aside as Ireland went soccer mad. This was the biggest match in the history of the nation, and we were playing the host nation on their home patch.

I led the Irish team out of the dressingroom and we lined up beside the Italians. They were waiting for us to take the long walk out onto the pitch together.

The Italians were jumping about, there was heavy breathing and stretching and messing with hair and boots – all signs of nerves. I turned to our own lads and said: 'Look at them – they're not too happy at all! They're very nervous, not looking forward to what they're going to get out there. Let's go and do them.'

I had come a long way in my career to this – leading the Republic of Ireland as captain. It had all started in my home town of Barnsley, thirty-one years earlier, and no matter where I travel to earn my living the town will always be important to me.

It's important for family reasons. For Barnsley is where my father, Charles McCarthy, settled after emigrating from Tallow in Waterford, met my mother, Josephine, a wonderful Yorkshire lady, got married and settled down. I think my father moved to Barnsley to try and find work down the pits. Back in the 50s, the town was surrounded by mines. It was boom time underground and every breadwinner seemed to work mining coal.

But the days of following your father down the pit are gone now. It all changed after pit closures and the year-long miners' strike in the early 80s. The industry has been decimated. There is something like 25 per cent or more unemployment in the area now.

I might have ended up down the pits if it hadn't been for football. But I wouldn't have been following my father. He got clever and took a job as a driver with an engineering firm and is now driving for the

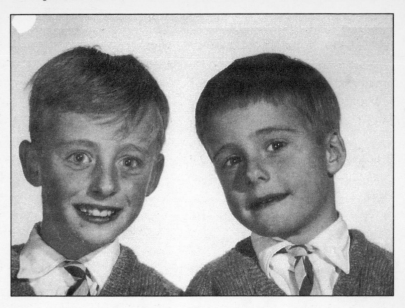

Above: DEADLY DUO – That's me on the right with my brother John. As you can see I couldn't tie a knot in my necktie ... some things never change!

Below: TERRIBLE THREESOME – this is me on the left with my sister Catherine and brother Kevin.

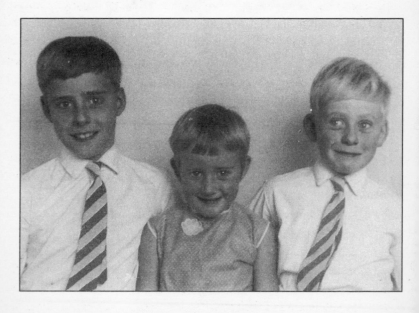

local social services.

Yet despite the strike and closures, which still affect many families in the area, that famous Yorkshire resilience always comes shining through. Adversity only draws Yorkshire people closer together. They remind me a lot of Irish people – friendly to the point that when a stranger comes to town they think we're nosey. Barnsley folk will make a point of asking you how you're doing. You arrive and they're across the street knocking on your door wanting to know if you need anything – do you want a cuppa, can they help? It's not being nosey, just friendly and helpful.

So this is the warm and caring atmosphere that first my eldest brother John, then myself, our kid brother, Kevin, and the baby of the family, Catherine, were born into. It's also the place where my wife, Fiona, was born – a year before me. I first met her when I was a mature four-year-old! Fiona has Irish blood too. Her grandparents lived in Athlone where her granddad was pensioned out of the Irish army, and her mother was born on the Curragh, another army garrison.

As a youngster growing up I was very aware of my Irishness. My Dad would tell us we were half-Irish. But we never went back to see the other part of my family in Waterford. It was hard enough to get my father out of the house, so what chance had we of getting him to take us to Tallow?

When I was about five the family moved out of the centre of Barnsley to a suburb called Worsbrough, where our family home still is. Before long I found myself at Our Lady's Junior School where I stayed until I was eleven.

SCHOOLBOY FOOTBALL

The first organised football I played was under the caring eye of the headmaster at Our Lady's, Mr Taylor. I remember with some trepidation the day we found out that he was leaving – to be replaced by a headmistress, Ms Kitchen. Panic set in. What would a woman know about football?

And then some of my pals got it up for me by telling me that she was thinking of drafting me into the netball team because I was tall. There were a couple of sleepless nights spent mulling over that one. But Ms Kitchen was doing nothing of the sort. The only drafting she

*A RIGHT PAIR OF COWBOYS – That's me on Yankee and my
big brother John, on a family holiday. Note the way I'm hanging
on for dear life.*

did was 'volunteering' the local parish priest, Fr Waller, and several
parents to help run the team.

Fr Waller was a real fan of the team. He'd come in at lunchtime,
take off his coat and collar and join us in a game of ball. He followed
us everywhere and helped out as much as he could in his spare time.
His commitment was never really rewarded. Our Lady's was a small
school, perhaps a hundred pupils, and we enjoyed our football though

*CAPED CRUSADER – Well, not really. This is Mick McCarthy on
his First Holy Communion day. Note the knobbly knees.*

we never won anything of importance.

But that all changed when Barnsley Juniors, the club's Under-11
team, asked me if I wanted to play. I joined near the end of the season
(1969/70) and played in the last eleven games. My 'career' with the
local Football League club had begun.

IT'S THE PITS – That's me on the left – with the beard – with my former boss Allan Clarke (right) after a visit to a local pit in South Yorkshire. Also in the picture are my former Barnsley teammates Peter Springett and Gary Pearce.

When I was eleven I moved on to Worsbrough High School which was considerably bigger with perhaps ten times the number of pupils. The choice of sports was considerable too, from canoeing to volleyball, cricket, rugby, tennis, athletics. You name it, Whitecross – the nickname given to the school because of the emblem on our blazers – had it. Football, however, was still the most important sport.

In my third year, when I was thirteen, I managed to get a trial for Barnsley Boys, which was a step up from the club's juniors. It was the usual thing at Barnsley trials – everybody was eligible. Hundreds of kids turned up. They had to get the numbers down to a squad of about twenty-two and then they would slowly cut it down to eighteen and finally sixteen. And the squad was always picked the same way. If you were around six foot and beginning to show signs of growing a beard (at fourteen) you had every chance of making the final squad!

I was in-between. Five foot ten with half a beard. I played in a few games up until the final sixteen and then I was asked to play up-front. Yes, me, up there trying to score goals as a centre-forward. The selectors had read about a McCarthy knocking in the goals for a local boys' club and naturally thought it was me. I wasn't about to tell them that it was my brother!

It didn't work out too well. Even though I scored, I played a stinker and, like my fellow schoolmates Peter Bergan and Dave Gledhill, I found myself on the scrapheap. A soccer reject at fourteen!

When we recovered from the being dumped by Barnsley Boys we drifted into local club teams. It was there that I met Keith Steele, the first person to take me under his wing and teach me a few things about the game, the way it should be played.

I was with Keith until I was sixteen. He coached me through my formative years after the disappointment of missing out with Barnsley Boys. And I achieved my first bit of success with his teams, playing in the Under-14s 15s, and 16s, usually winning a trophy at the end of each season.

And Keith would occasionally stick me into the Under-18 team. I'd struggle, but it gave me a lot of experience playing against what I thought of then as grown men. I owe Keith Steele a great deal for all his help in those early years. If he hadn't taken me under his wing it might have gone very sour for me.

By now schoolwork was suffering, badly suffering – and I never really caught up. Soccer was now the most important thing to me. I was only in the door at weekends to have a bite to eat and it was: 'Goodbye, Mum. Can you wash this kit? I'm playing again in the morning.' It was the school team on Saturday morning. The Worsbrough Miners' Welfare Saturday afternoon, Swaithe Miners' Welfare Sunday morning, and the Boys' Club Sunday afternoon.

Needless to say the Boys' Club never got everything out of me until I actually stopped playing with the Welfare teams. Yet I had a great deal of success with them until I was sixteen. Then decisions had to be made. And the biggest one wasn't too hard. My schooldays were over, and I left Worsbrough with not too many qualifications. Now I was destined to go to the pit as an apprentice electrician. The only thing that might stop me from spending the rest of my life working in the local colliery was football.

I had by now managed to get a few games for Barnsley's reserves. They were reasonably happy with me I thought when I started to keep some first-team players out of the reserves. Then Keith Steele told me that Barnsley were interested. His father, who was secretary of the club, had told him. But he also said that Barnsley manager, Jim Iley, for some mysterious reason, just didn't want to ask me! I had to move quickly. The pre-selection test for the apprentice electrician's job had been passed and I was waiting for my call-up. I went to see Jim Iley. I just went in and asked him would he sign me – and he said Yes.

APPRENTICE AT BARNSLEY

So in December 1973 I joined Barnsley Football Club as an apprentice footballer on the princely sum of £14 a week. I would have been on £35 at the pit. That's probably the main reason I wanted to go there. Anyway, thank God I never did. For my first pay packet I had to work a week in hand. As I said I joined for the princely sum of fourteen quid a week and when I left the club, almost ten years later, I never picked up that back week. So Barnsley Football Club still owe me £14!

So began ten smashing years with the local team, learning my profession. And it wasn't all football either. No, there was no pampering youngsters at Oakwell, especially sixteen-year-olds who sometimes thought they knew it all. There was time for kicking a ball in the Northern Intermediate League and the odd game in the reserves. But there were also all the other jobs to be done. You name it and the apprentices had to do it. The club professionals' boots had to be cleaned, divots had to be replaced in the pitch, terraces swept, and barriers painted. The young lads were general dogsbodies and gofers.

But I don't think I would have changed any of it. Not one detail –

well, maybe when it came to flushing out the toilet at the back of the terrace!

Very soon after I was taken on as an apprentice, the groundsman, Norman Rimmington, appointed me head apprentice. I think Norman gave me the job simply because I was the biggest, and to keep me quiet! I used to get into scrapes with some of the first teamers, or maybe one of the management staff, because I was prone to shout my mouth off.

Norman Rimmington did his bit to keep my feet on the ground. Norm had been around Oakwell for years. Somewhere in the distant past he had played for the club. Since then he has done everything else and is still there as groundsman now. He would pull me aside and tell me to cool down if I was blowing my top. He would watch me play and give me some useful advice. But if I wasn't doing my job as head apprentice, Norman would let me know soon enough as well. When I go back home to Barnsley these days I always try and look up some of my old friends. A trip down to Oakwell for a cuppa with Norman is always high on the list.

The footballing side of my game was developing too, in between becoming a master decorator and groundsman! We played our football on the Queen's ground, opposite Oakwell. And although Barnsley were in the Fourth Division, we always seemed to have a crop of good youngsters.

We did well in the Intermediate League. It was a tough league for Under-19s and I'm afraid only the strongest survived. We were all pushing for positions – and our future – playing against teams like Sheffield United, Sheffield Wednesday, Leeds, Newcastle and Middlesbrough.

Barnsley was the perfect place to learn your trade. The following season, 1974, we got to the final of the Northern Intermediate League Cup and then won the League. We lost the Cup but went on to win the League on a couple more occasions after that.

After two years playing in the Intermediate League I felt I was ready for my Football League debut and a place in the first team. I thought that I would make my debut at the beginning of the 1977/78 season. But the boss, Jim Iley, had other ideas. I don't think Jim and I hit it off that well. Maybe it was because I was too forthright and outspoken for him. Jim probably thought I was a cheeky brat, and he was probably right. But ironically enough, when Jim left to take over at Blackburn Rovers he was on the phone the same week trying to buy me!

I was getting a little impatient that I wasn't getting into the first team in the 1977/78 season. Jim kept telling the newspapers that he was going to throw in some of the youngsters, but it wasn't happening. So I started the season in the reserves. I can't say I was happy but as an eighteen-year-old on the books of a Fourth Division club who hadn't made his Football League debut yet I was in no position to walk in and demand a transfer!

ON THE FIRST TEAM

I was counting the hours to when I would actually rub shoulders with the men in the first team. I knew that it would happen sometime. But when it came I was shocked.

With just a couple of League matches played in the 77/78 season, we were down to play Chesterfield in the League Cup. John Saunders, a seasoned campaigner with Barnsley, and Peter Burke, who had been around the club for a few seasons, were playing at the centre of the defence. We were beaten 4-1 – pulled a consolation goal back in the final few minutes. In the second leg, at Oakwell, Jim Iley finally decided to throw me into the team.

The boss told me about ninety minutes before the game. I remember it well. The first thing I did was run to the local post office to telephone Fiona that I was about to make my debut. But, as usual, the phone was engaged!

It was an evening kick-off. I got to the ground early and some of the older lads made me feel welcome and wished me all the best. The game couldn't have gone better for me. I scored the first goal. We won 3-0, matching Chesterfield's first-leg score, and the game went into extra time. No more goals though, so we went to a replay.

I got some good write-ups in the papers over the following days ... and Jim Iley told the press that he always knew I was going to make it but that I had to keep my feet on the ground. All the usual stuff a manager says about a young player. He kept me in the team then for the next game, my League debut against Rochdale, Saturday, August

20, 1977. We won that one 4-0. I had finally arrived at the age of eighteen years, six months and thirteen days!

I didn't miss a game for the rest of the season and I still remember the team that played in my League debut to this day: Peter Springett, Barrie Murphy, John Collins, Graham Pugh, John Saunders, Mick McCarthy, Alan Little, Peter Price, John Peachey, Graham Collier and Neill Warnock. Sub: Brian Joicey.

What was particularly pleasing that season was the fact that my critics were expecting me to blow up and get dropped. But I stuck to the job that had to be done and played forty-six League matches.

Around the end of that season – we finished seventh behind Watford, Southend, Swansea, Brentford, Aldershot and Grimsby – I went in to see Jim Iley to try and get some more money. Jim explained that he couldn't give me any more than £60 as an eighteen-year-old single man, otherwise it might upset some of the older professionals with families.

Soon afterwards Jim was gone – and then he telephoned me from Blackburn Rovers and offered me £100 a week! It was probably at that moment I realised how devious professional football can be, how strange and fickle.

Anyway, I signed a new contract with Barnsley with the chairman and General Secretary, Johnny Steele. He told me that they had some young guy coming in as manager, an ambitious young fella who was a former England international. I hadn't got a clue who it was at the time but when he walked through the door I was gobsmacked. It was Allan Clarke, 'Sniffer', the former Leeds United and England striker.

Allan was great for Barnsley. He was like a breath of fresh air blowing through the club, with a whole new attitude to the game, particularly off the pitch. He was the first guy who stopped us bringing our kit home to be washed. Yes, even at a Football League club then we had to bring our dirty, mucky gear home. Mum was more than happy about that. Allan got us into club outfits, made us feel like First Division players – and his ideas paid off that season.

I played in every game and we finished fourth to win promotion to Division Three. My first success in the Football League. It was a great season. Allan put some pride back into the town when it came to the football team and the fans came back in their droves. We were used to three, four or maybe five thousand passing through the turnstiles. Now the crowds for games against other Yorkshire teams were up to ten and eleven thousand. And in our final game of that 78/79 season we had 21,261 fans at Oakwell to see us win promotion.

Then, as a reward for winning promotion, we were all taken off to Marbella for an end-of-season break. Allan was behind that too. It was my first time in a plane. A whole new experience, terrific.

To cap it all, my fellow professionals voted me onto the PFA Fourth Division Awards team.

1979/80 SEASON

The euphoria of winning promotion soon disappeared at the beginning of the 79/80 season. We started badly and continued to struggle for a time.

Allan Clarke moved in October to try and bring some stability to the team. He contacted Bristol City and made an offer for his former club and international teammate Norman Hunter. Nobody for one minute thought that Norman, one of my own great heroes, would come to Barnsley. But Allan Clarke can be very persuasive and three months into the season Hunter arrived at Oakwell.

When I was a little younger I used to watch Norman Hunter, Allan Clarke – and Jack Charlton – play for Leeds United. The great Leeds United team of the 70s. Now Clarke was my boss and I was playing alongside Norman Hunter at Barnsley.

My only disappointment was that I didn't get to play too many times with Norman. He was injured after a few games and was out of the team but when he was playing I just wanted to learn everything I could from him. We found some form shortly after Norman's arrival and we gradually hauled ourselves into a safe, mid-table position in Division Three.

By March 1980 Clarke was already building for the following season. He convinced the board of directors that we would have to splash out on some new players and they agreed to release some money to buy. Allan almost broke the bank when he paid out £95,000 for Ian Evans, the Crystal Palace defender. He also acquired the services of two strikers – Trevor Aylott from Chelsea and Ronnie Glavin from Glasgow Celtic. It was some measure of Clarke's influence and ability to sell Barnsley that he could convince players of that calibre to make the move to an unfashionable place like Barnsley.

Ian Evans was soon in the team playing alongside me. We were to play many a game together and I once again got an education from another player with a lot of experience. Ian was a steadying influence on me. A bad injury finally ended his playing career some years later but we still remain great friends. Now, I'm happy to say, we have been re-united at Millwall where Ian is on the coaching staff.

We had a good little run towards the end of that season and there was a real buzz at the club during the summer that we could make a challenge for promotion to Division Two in 1980/81.

1980/81 SEASON

We got off to a great start in August and September 1980. But then we lost Allan Clarke after about a month. Allan's team-building and general professional approach to the game had been noticed by several clubs, and when Leeds United were looking out for a new manager they decided that Allan was the man for them. The club didn't stand in his way. Allan felt he could re-awaken a sleeping giant at Elland Road. One of the biggest jobs in football was to take Leeds back into the First Division.

Barnsley decided to replace Allan from within – and there was only one real choice, Norman Hunter. It was a choice that delighted every player, particularly me, as I had got on with Norman exceptionally well. Norman didn't make major changes. He just took over from Allan and kept everything on an even keel. I think he knew that if we could just continue where we left off the previous season we might win promotion. He was right, we finished second. It was one of the best Barnsley teams I have ever played in. A well-balanced side with some great ball players and plenty of grit at the back. Our success came on the back of a tremendous unbeaten run beginning on October 4, 1980. We seemed to be invincible until we went down to Reading and lost 2-3 on January 31.

And at the end of the season there was another players' award to go on the mantelpiece when Ian Evans, Ronnie Glavin and myself were named in the Division Three team for 1980/81. There was also an end-of-season trip to Florida.

TAKE IT OUT OF THE NET, SEAMUS – This is what it was all about at Barnsley, getting in a good header against Bolton Wanderers to score (1980/81). The goalkeeper that day was Seamus McDonagh, my former Irish teammate.

1981/82 SEASON

Barnsley was now a 'big' club. We were in Division Two, possibly a season away from the First Division. And we could have won promotion in 1981/82. In some ways we blew it. We became somewhat full of our own importance. We finished sixth, which was disappointing, very disappointing. We had a good team then. A team that WAS capable of winning a place in Division One.

Part of our problem that season could have been money. Self-importance can make you feel that you're worth more than what you're getting. Clubs, of course, always try to peg you back when it comes to talking money. But maybe some players got a little too greedy.

While promotion for the second consecutive season slipped away from us we did have a great run in the League Cup.

A 9-2, two-leg aggregate victory over Peterborough in the first round was followed by an exciting two-leg clash with Swansea. We beat the Swans at home 2-0, but then they scored two against us at the Vetch Field and the game went to extra time – I think it was Ian Banks who scored a late goal that allowed us to squeeze through 5-4 on aggregate.

We drew Brighton in the third round and hammered them 4-1 at Oakwell, with yours truly scoring one of his rare goals. But it was the last sixteen of the competition that really set the town alight.

We were drawn to meet Manchester City at our place, and within a week of the draw over 25,000 tickets had been sold for the match. The night we played them I just couldn't believe the crowd. And with 33,792 crammed into Oakwell, we reached the last eight with a 1-0 victory.

The quarter-finals saw us pitted against Liverpool, again over two legs. And when we managed to hold the mighty Reds to a goalless draw at Anfield we really fancied our chances of getting a result back at our place. Maybe we were a little complacent in the second match. Maybe we forgot the old saying that Liverpool are at their most dangerous when they seem to be down, but we learned our lesson – they won 3-1.

1982/83 SEASON

We seemed to have lost our bite at the First Division cherry because the following season we finished tenth. We peaked in fifth position in March and then blew it. The most notable highlight was the fact that Ian Evans was made coach at the club.

I thought long and hard about my position with Barnsley that season. I was happy enough there. The club had been good to me. But I felt that if I wanted to improve myself I might have to consider getting away.

TRANSFER

Shortly after the start of the 1983/84 season I found myself suspended. Nicky Law came in, played very well as my replacement, and the boss had to keep him in. I was dismayed. I had never experienced this before, being dropped.

I tried to take the decision with my usual dignity – before I walked in and asked for a transfer! I missed about seven or eight games before I finally got back into the team. But I knew then that several clubs had heard on the grapevine that I was unhappy, and the home fixture against Chelsea on December 10 proved to be my last game for Barnsley.

I heard that Newcastle had made some enquiries but nothing came of that, and then Manchester City showed some interest. Out of the blue one morning secretary Johnny Steele told me that Barnsley and Manchester City had discussed a fee. Everything happened very quickly. I went over to Manchester and discussed the move with manager Billy McNeill. Then it was back into the car over the Pennines to Barnsley to discuss the move with my wife Fiona. I didn't need too much convincing. City were a big club, one of the biggest in England. Like Leeds they were another sleeping giant. The differences between Oakwell and Maine Road were tremendous.

Billy McNeill impressed me a lot. He had been the captain of Glasgow Celtic when they won the European Champions Cup back in 1967 and had won every major honour north of the border as a player and manager. I finally signed for City on December 13 in a £200,000 transfer deal and was in the team to play Cambridge on the Saturday.

MANCHESTER CITY

THE FIRST THING I REMEMBER about City was the number of Scots around the club. Billy McNeill, of course, was the boss. But then his assistant Jimmy Frizzell, Gordon Dalziel, Neil McNab, Derek Parlane, Asa Hartford and Jim Tolmie were all from north of the border.

We drew with Cambridge 1-1 on my debut, but the immediate fixture I was looking forward to came a few weeks later – my return to Barnsley, in a City jersey.

It was a strange feeling going back to Oakwell. Now I was changing in the visitors' dressingroom. I saw some of my former teammates before that match and we exchanged pleasantries but I knew that as soon as I ran out on to the pitch I would be trying to put one over on them.

On reflection the result, a 1-1 draw, was probably the best one for me. The fans didn't give me the hard time I had expected and afterwards some of them even came up to me and wished me all the best at City.

It didn't take me long to become something of a favourite with the City fans either. For although I played only twenty-four games that season after signing in December, and we missed out on promotion by finishing fourth, they voted me Player of the Year.

MY FIRST INTERNATIONAL

Then came one of the biggest moments in my whole career. Billy McNeill called me in one morning and told me that Eoin Hand, then manager of the Republic of Ireland, had made enquiries and wanted to know if I was available to play.

When I wanted to leave Barnsley to better myself I never thought I would end up playing international football. And with Dave O'-Leary, Mark Lawrenson and Kevin Moran all available to play for Ireland, I never thought I'd ever make it into their squad – never mind play. But being with a club like City, one with a high profile, I had been noticed. I don't think it would have happened at Barnsley.

Eoin called me up for a friendly against Poland in May 1984 to be followed by a trip to Japan where the Republic had been invited to play in a tournament in Sapporo. I hesitated. My brother John was getting married just about that time and I was due to be his best man. 'Well, do you want to come or what?' Eoin asked. 'Sure, when do you want me over?' I said, knowing well enough that I would be in the dog house with my wife Fiona and my family. Another wedding missed. But I thought that if I was lucky I might get a dozen or so caps for the Republic and this was a chance to earn some more. The following Sunday, May 20, I flew over from Manchester and joined the rest of the squad at the Green Isle Hotel which was the team's headquarters at the time. It was all very laid back. I met the rest of the players that evening and soon settled into the squad. But I thought at the time that at best I would be a cover player. How could I think any other way with the likes of Mark Lawrenson, David O'Leary and

Kevin Moran in the squad?

While for the many the game on Wednesday was a non-event, for me it was very special – my international debut. The match was one of those end-of-the-season friendlies with nothing at stake, and it ended 0-0. The highlight for me was playing against Zbigniew Boniek. He had burst onto the international scene a couple of years earlier at the 1982 World Cup finals in Spain. So I rounded off a wonderful season that night at Dalymount with my first cap. I thought that I had played reasonably well.

In Japan, and Eoin chose me to play against China on Sunday, June 3, 1984. It was the first time I'd seen Chinese men over six foot, I didn't think they made them that big. Their team ranged from a little fellow that kicked me on the knee, to two center-halves that towered over me. We won that match 1-0 but I had taken a knock which ruled me out of the final against SC International from Brazil.

1984/85 SEASON

The new season dawned, with everybody connected with Manchester City confident that we could win promotion.

Days before the season kicked off, Billy McNeill appointed me captain. I 'rewarded' him by getting booked in my first game as skipper! Billy was furious. He pulled me aside and told me that I was probably the worst guy he could have made skipper. Being the cool, calm and collected type, I soon told Billy where he could stick his captaincy … Yet Billy had a point. I had a crazy start to the season, getting booked on several occasions and ending up suspended in October. And on the day I returned to the team I got booked again!

But I settled down after that – until the third last game of the season at Portsmouth. Promotion was staring us in the face and I was going to have to sit it out on the bench. In the penultimate match we lost 3-1 to Notts County. Now we had to beat Charlton at home to make sure of promotion – and Nicky Reid and myself were suspended. And to make a point the lads went out and ran riot, winning 5-1!

Maine Road was packed with over 50,000 fans who went wild. City, and Mick McCarthy, were in the First Division. Unbelievably, I also got voted into the Second Division awards team at the end of that season as well.

OUCH! – I don't know who felt this one more, United's Mark Hughes or myself, in this United-City derby clash at Maine Road, September 1985.

1985/86

I thought the new season, 1985/86, would never come around quick enough. I was like a baby looking forward to playing in the First Division. I would have loved to do it with Barnsley. But I was there with Manchester City and that was fine by me.

However, I had a nightmare beginning to the season. We played Wimbledon in our first game. They had won promotion with us and we drew 2-2. Soon after that I found myself playing in one of Britain's great derby matches, City vs. United. We began well enough – until I sent a suicidal back pass in the direction of our 'keeper Alex Williams. Alex hadn't a chance and he had to pull down a United player and give away a penalty which they duly converted.

The fans were not too happy with me. My nightmare went on from there. I scored an own goal at home playing against West Ham – then another against Southampton!

The West Ham goal was something special, very spectacular. I slid in at the far post, caught the rest of my defence off guard and finished it off the way only a top-class striker can. The one against Southampton just hit me and was deflected past our goalkeeper, a nonsense goal.

My nightmare continued. The more I tried to get things right the worse I seemed to get. The turning point came when we played Fourth Division Bury in the Cup. The ball came through a ruck of players like a bullet and hit me in the arm. No own goal this time – just a penalty which they converted.

After that, I thought: Well bugger it, it can't be all my fault. It's got to be a bit of bad luck, so in the next game, at Oxford, I went back to basics. John Aldridge was in their team then, along with Billy Hamilton. I kept the promise I made to myself before the game and began doing the simple things properly. It worked, and I got back on the rails. After that I was reasonably happy with my performance for the second half of the season. Nothing spectacular mind you, just finally finding my feet at that level.

We lost to United at Maine Road but made up for it somewhat by holding them to 2-2 in a brilliant match at Old Trafford. The weekend of that match was particularly hectic for City. Soon after the draw we had to head down the motorway to London to meet Chelsea in the Full Members Cup final the next day at Wembley. That was a crazy, crazy game. We took the lead but ended up losing 5-4. Great entertainment for the fans, but even better if we had won. An old mate at Barnsley, David Speedie, destroyed us by scoring a hat-trick. How would you feel if one of your best friends went and stitched you up at Wembley?

The Wembley trip was a nice break for us. It helped take our minds off the League for a weekend. It had been a struggle all season, a rearguard battle to stay in the First Division. We managed to win it and finished 15th – but, sadly, the war was to be lost the following season.

1986/87 SEASON

Things began to turn sour at City from the opening of the 1986/87 season. For a start, Billy McNeill, the man who had given me my big chance with City and taken me into the First Division, decided to leave the club and join Aston Villa. Billy left after just two games I think. We had become good friends. A strong mutual respect had grown between us and I admired him a lot. I wished him the best of luck – little did I know that our paths would cross again in the very near future.

Jimmy Frizzell took over. But I think even Jimmy knew that we were going to have a real battle on our hands to stay up. He brought in goalkeeper Perry Suckling and the experienced England defender John Gidman.

Some of the City youngsters were also given a chance. Players like Ian Brightwell had a baptism of fire in Division One. Then my old Irish teammate Stumpy – Tony Grealish – arrived. I had had some great battles with Stumpy when he was with Brighton and now I was glad he was playing for us. Paul Stewart (now at Tottenham) and Imre Varadi, also known as Oliver Ardi The Flying Turk, tried to do their best to keep us in the top flight. We had a great bunch of lads, a fair old drinking squad – we just couldn't play football!

Ironically I felt that I played well that season and relegation was heartbreaking. It was the first time I had been with a team that had gone down. I couldn't face that. I had played my nuts off for eight years trying to get to a big club in the First Division and I wasn't about to go back to the Second. I talked to the boss and told him. If a decent offer came in at the end of the season I wanted to go. It was as simple as that.

TRANSFER

Near the end of the season several clubs approached City about a possible move. The club needed to balance their books and they were rubbing their hands over it. To be fair to Jimmy Frizzell he didn't want me to go. But Billy McNeill had told me once that if City could get a good price for their goal posts then they would sell them!

Apparently Sheffield Wednesday were the first club to show an interest. But Wednesday had made several enquiries for me when I was at Barnsley and never put their money where their mouth was. Then rumours abounded about a possible move to Liverpool. I didn't believe Jimmy when he told me that. But then he said that Wednesday would be outbid by Liverpool – and then Glasgow Celtic entered the race and it became an auction. City lapped it up.

Jimmy was in his element. He is one of the best wheeler-dealers in the business when it comes to buying players at bargain prices and selling them for small fortunes. He did it again with me. He managed to get Celtic to agree to a fee of £500,000. I don't believe I was worth that much, but anyway I wasn't too disappointed. It had nothing to do with me, what they paid for me, so long as I got a good move.

Fiona and I drove up from our home in Wilmslow, Cheshire, to Glasgow one day in May 1987 to talk over personal terms. I'll never forget that journey. It rained most of the way and having left the leafy avenues of Wilmslow for the grime of a dirty old town like Glasgow I wondered was I making the right decision.

But one look around Parkhead – the history of the place, the plans that manager David Hay had for the coming season and the feeling for the club in Glasgow – and I knew I just had to sign.

Manchester City had been good to me and I'm as pleased as punch that they are now back in Division One. What many people might not realise is that while being a big club City is still very homely, much more so than United.

Manchester City – great memories, grateful that they had taken me to a big club and into the spotlight. But now I was on may way to Celtic, a bigger club, one of the biggest in Europe.

CELTIC

THE FIRST SHOCK AFTER I SIGNED FOR CELTIC was the high profile players have in Glasgow and the surrounding areas. There are other teams around the city and its environs but Celtic and Rangers are what it's all about. The two clubs – known to everyone as the 'Old Firm' – make a big thing of signing new players. There's a lot of razzmatazz involved and by the end of the day, after putting pen to paper, you're a new hero to half the city and a sworn enemy of the other.

I don't think there's another city in Britain where soccer means so much to people. Glaswegians take everything at their respective clubs deadly seriously. After just a couple of days, before I had even played a game, the fans were coming up to me, grasping my hand firmly and wishing me all the best for the coming season. At the same time Rangers fans were already sick of seeing my ugly mug in the papers and hearing my name on the radio! When I ran into some of them it was: 'Ah you Fenian bastard', and other such pleasantries.

The first time that happened to me I was a little shocked to say the least. As I drove home after my first encounter with these bigoted supporters I vowed that I'd never get involved with them if they tried to goad me – because no matter what happened I wou!d come out of it in a bad light. It would be so easy to answer them with a punch, but that doesn't sort anything out. It just makes the situation worse. Just let them live in their squalid bigotry. I was also warned that I could be picked out for special attention by some of Rangers' most rabid fans because not only had I joined Celtic but I was now playing regularly for the Republic of Ireland and that was like a red rag to a bull with them.

Being the stubborn man that I am, the abuse had made me more than just a Celtic player, I was becoming a staunch Celt and I hadn't even kicked a ball for them yet! So what if I was a dirty Fenian bastard? Why should that bother me, so long as nobody started to insult me when Fiona and the kids were around. They could call me what they liked when I was by myself, I was getting well paid for it. I was mature enough to take it now – and I thanked God that I wasn't twenty-one because my reactions might have been a little different.

When I reported for training for my first season at Celtic in July 1987, the manager David Hay was gone – the man who sold me on Celtic and signed me had now been given the push. I had joined the club in May for £500,000 after meeting David in a hotel in Carlisle and agreeing terms. Eight days later I was in Luxembourg playing for the Republic in a European Championship qualifying match. After the match in the dressingroom I was aware of a commotion in the corridor. Mick Byrne, the physio, was shouting at the press men to get away from our dressingroom door. Then he came in and told me that David Hay had been sacked. My first thoughts were the lesson to be learned by every other manager – don't sign Mick McCarthy for £500,000 or you just might lose your job three days later! But then I heard who the new manager was and I rested a little easier. Billy McNeill was back at Parkhead. Just as well I had had a good relationship with Billy during my years at Manchester City.

However, I didn't have the best of starts under Billy at Celtic. We went away in July to Sweden for pre-season training and a few friendly matches. I wasn't long training when I tore a stomach muscle which was a real pain in the ass. I was so looking forward to playing for the Celts. I was struggling and didn't play in any of the friendlies. I soldiered on to try and get my fitness back but my injuries lasted for twelve weeks! Just as the stomach injury cleared up I tore a calf muscle. And the jokes started to go the rounds. The fans were saying that Celtic hadn't signed Mick McCarthy at all! It was just a big wind-up. I was, they said, off riding Shergar with Lord Lucan!

ON THE FIELD AT LAST

Then, finally, after those twelve weeks of jokes and jibes I made my debut for the Celts in a UEFA Cup tie in West Germany. I thought I played quite well against Borusia Dortmund even though we were beaten 2-1. I was happy, considering the amount of games I had missed through injury. Now I was looking forward to making my debut in the Scottish League against Hibs on the Saturday.

But what a personal nightmare that turned out to be. I felt good up to half-time, and we were winning 1-0. The pace of the game surprised me however, and after about ten minutes of the second half I was totally knackered, the worst I have ever felt in a match. With the score at 1-1, Billy saved me from any more anguish by taking me off. Not the best introduction to the Scottish Premier League. The fans wanted to know why Celtic had bought such a dumpling.

But Billy kept faith in me. And after a few more games and a couple of runs in the reserves, I found my feet and ended up playing twenty-three games in the League. The fans were happy with me now. And why shouldn't they be because Celtic were heading for the title and Rangers didn't beat us that season.

One of those 'Old Firm' games has gone down in history. The game was played at a packed Ibrox stadium on October 17. We had gone two goals up and were coasting when Frank McAvennie was involved in a tussle for the ball with the Rangers goalkeeper Chris Woods. The next thing war has broken out down that end of the field and after spending five minutes sorting it out the referee sent off Woods, McAvennie and the Rangers captain, Terry Butcher. The following day the law was involved, with charges of almost inciting a riot being levelled at Butcher! Crazy game really, two-up when there were twenty-two players on the pitch, 2-2 with only nineteen on!

CELTIC-RANGERS HATRED

While that particular derby game made the headlines right across the world for all the wrong reasons, it was the clash at Ibrox on January 2, 1988 that brought home to me the full extent of the sickening bigotry that exists in Glasgow. At the time I was suspended. Just before the kick-off Peter Grant and I took our seats in the Rangers director's box. Peter, born and reared a Celt, was the most hated man in the stand because he was the epitomy of all that Celtic stood for. It was a tense game and then Celtic took the lead. Peter and I jumped up to celebrate the goal. That wasn't something you do as a Celtic fan in the director's box at Rangers. A mistake – a BIG mistake.

We got some funny looks but nobody said anything. Then Rangers equalised through Jan Bartram and the whole place erupted. Now it started – the Rangers fans began spitting at us. It was incredible. I had never seen anything like it in my life. The hate in their eyes, real hate, I thought they were going to climb over the seats and beat us to death. I don't think I have ever been so frightened in my life at a football match. But the lads on the field had the last laugh. We took the lead and Peter and I were on our feet again as the team hung on to win.

After that match I had another worry. Lex Baillie had come in to replace me and he had a great game. I had done well up to then – the defence was playing brilliantly and we had conceded only twelve goals all season. The Scottish Cup final was looming on the horizon and I desperately wanted to play in that. It was my own fault of course. I had lost my place through suspension and now I was struggling to get back into the team as Celtic chased the double.

SCOTTISH CHAMPIONSHIP/CUP DOUBLE

Then, with just two or three games to go before the Cup final, we were playing at Hearts and we were beaten 2-1. I was the happiest man in the crowd. Don't get me wrong, I was a Celt now and you always want to see your team win. But it meant that I had a chance to win my place back for the Cup final. Billy had pulled me aside a few days earlier and was honest about the situation. The team were playing well. He couldn't change a winning side. Now they had been beaten and the door was open for me to return.

We were trying to wrap up the Championship before the final at Hampden and I was part of things again. We played Dundee and beat them and that victory won us the Championship. The celebrations began but I didn't feel part of it. I had only played about twenty-one or twenty-two games up to that, in and out of the team through injury and suspension. But it was wonderful that day at Parkhead. Over 50,000 fans to celebrate our success.

We went away for a few days before the final to Sea Mill Hydro where we usually got together before big games. We had had a wonderful season, crushed almost everybody and now we were hot favourites to win the Cup and complete the double. Only Dundee United stood between us and it.

It was a red-hot day at Hampden for the final and we took time to settle. It's a matter of fact that United started better than us, but at half-time it was still 0-0. Then, not long after we resumed battle, United struck and took the lead through Kevin Gallacher, a striker who had been a Celtic supporter all his life. We had been all over them but just couldn't score. Then time began to slip by and into the last fifteen minutes I began to think it's not going to be our day. Frank

McAvennie had other ideas. With ten minutes remaining, he tied the match and then with almost the last kick of the game he won the Cup for us. Hampden went wild. Wonderful scene. I had never experienced such emotion, such love for a club. I had experienced a little success south of the border in my promotion years with Barnsley and City, but now I was at Hampden getting a real winner's medal and holding the Scottish Cup with the lads. I was a double winner.

THE CELTIC TRADITION

And the fans chanted all our names. They cried with happiness. I couldn't believe it. They loved us, they loved Parkhead and anything at all to do with Celtic. Many of them live, breathe, eat and drink the place. A fair chunk of their wages goes on their first love – Celtic. They bring their youngsters from an early age and get them immersed in the tradition of it all. And once bitten by the bug few of them can ever get over it. If the 'Bhoys' won on a Saturday they'd have a smile as wide as the Forth Bridge when they went to work on Monday. If we lost, particularly to Rangers, they might not surface at their workplace for a few days.

I have been at a game when we have gone behind, and then up to 30,000 fans will all start singing 'You'll Never Walk Alone' to lift you. That's another special experience I'll never forget. It's something I have never seen anywhere else. If you pull on that green and white hooped shirt you are immediately an idol, placed on a pedestal. You are expected to perform for the Celts, and nothing but 100 per cent commitment will do. They expect that all the time, and they're entitled to it with what they have contributed to the club down through the years.

The players try and pay them back off the field as well. The fans would have all these presentation dances they expected us to go to. There they would hand out the Player of the Year awards for that particular branch of the supporters' club. After we did the double, Paul McStay was in big demand. Paul could have been out every night picking up awards and meeting the fans. And after a fitful start I had, I think, won a place in their hearts too. Playing for the Republic of Ireland helped as well because there is such a great link between Celtic fans and Ireland.

*HE FLEW THROUGH THE AIR – This is me in action at Parkhead.
With a shape like that I wouldn't go amiss at the Royal Ballet!*

1988/1989 SEASON

That summer I went off to Germany with Ireland for the European Championships, had a holiday with the family and returned for pre-season training feeling great and hoping to have a somewhat better start to 1988/89. I was bombing in training and played five-and-a-half games out of six in our friendlies.

But then I got a thigh muscle strain. It wasn't much and I travelled to Italy with the club for a tournament, but had to sit it out because of the injury. Yet when I came back I felt great and was in the team that defeated Hearts comfortably in our first League match of the season.

That was probably one of our best games of the season because we were destined to struggle in the League. Rangers had a worse start, but they managed to make a comeback with a vengeance and would eventually take the title.

Two or three weeks into the season we went up to Dundee United and we were knocking the ball around well. For some reason, however, I felt tired. Maybe the European Championships and a tough pre-season schedule had caught up on me. Anyway, with little danger about I decided to pass the ball back to Ian Andrews. I only half-hit the ball and there was Kevin Gallacher (again!) nipping in on the most perfect of passes to score for United.

Needless to say I was looking for a hole to dive into. I was trying to dig one – I was actually trying to pack the soil down on top of me! Of course the television cameras were there and it was shown all over the world for everybody to see. When I saw it on TV it made me feel an even bigger twat. But the Celtic fans were great that afternoon. They actually started singing 'There's only one Mick McCarthy'. Well, I think it was them – it might have been the Dundee United supporters who were singing it!

I tried my nuts off after that and actually had a great header saved in the last few minutes. I would have loved to have redeemed myself, but it wasn't to be. And of course I lost my head in that game, started running about like a headless chicken, kicking a few people. I eventually got booked for something that was quite innocuous and I was taken off. Billy was not impressed one bit. He said, 'Great isn't it? We sent three players (Packie Bonner, Chris Morris and myself) away to the European Championships to play their hearts out and they forgot to bring their game back to Celtic.' The boss was right. We were playing that badly.

I picked up a knock in that game, but that wouldn't have made any difference with Billy – I was out for the next match anyway. In fact I was dropped for a few matches and I wasn't happy. Billy knew it. I could never take being dropped no matter where I was, Barnsley Boys through to Celtic. I did play in the European Champions' Cup match in Hungary against Honved. We were beaten 1-0 and nobody played well.

Billy recalled me for the return leg at Parkhead and we took them apart 4-1. It was one of those great nights at Parkhead, a European Cup tie with the place packed with Celtic fans. We hammered them, gave them a battering. I felt part of the team again and had done enough to convince the boss that I should stay in. However, we were still struggling, dropping silly points and playing nowhere near as well as the previous season. What made it worse for our fans was that Rangers, who had already won the Skol League Cup, were beginning to move ahead in the race for the League Championship.

RUMOURS

Our last hope of glory that season was in the Scottish Cup and we had moved through the early rounds comfortably enough. Then, in the week leading up to our quarter-final clash with Hearts, I began to hear rumours that the French club, Olympique Lyon, were interested in me. Hours before the match I heard that representatives from Lyon were coming to watch me. At this stage I had decided that if I could get a move to the Continent and the terms were right I would go. You have to remember that a professional's career is very short in this game. You have to make the most of it, make as much money as you can while you're playing in order to safeguard the future of your family.

The French party were led for the day by Peter Boyle, a dermatologist working in Lyons for the World Health Organisation who happened to come from Glasgow and was a Celtic fanatic. They had enjoyed the day so far. They had been made welcome by the Celtic executives and had loved the atmosphere at Parkhead. The game began well for me. Hearts had stuck their midfielder Mike Galloway up-front to try and upset our defenders. I loved that – instead of Mike battering us I was battering him! He wasn't getting a look-in and then I headed this clearance all of fifty yards down the park. Mark McGhee was on it like a light and bang – it was in the back of the net.

Then we got a penalty. It was now 2-0 for Celtic. Hearts were on the rack and when their young fullback had words with the referee he found himself heading for an early bath. We were coasting two-up with an extra man on the pitch. The game began to get a little too physical, boot studs and elbows flying, but I had decided to stay well out of it. Both teams began to get stuck in, the tackles were flying everywhere. I didn't want to get into any bother with the party from Lyon watching me. The ball was played up to our midfielder, Billy Stark, and one of their lads just came in and hit him. It was one of the worst tackles I have ever seen – and I snapped, lost my cool.

I ran up the field towards the offender, my blood boiling. But he saw me coming and as I went to grab him he ducked out and I ended up on the ground. As I got up, two or three of my teammates grabbed and restrained me. The referee wasn't pleased, and even though I hadn't laid a finger on him we were both sent off. I have to admit that even to this day if I had got hold of him I probably would have knocked his block off. Only twenty-five minutes of the match had passed and I had made a goal and got sent off. I really thought I had blown my chances of joining a Continental club.

But Peter Boyle loved it all. He had been used to the blood and thunder of the British game – and the coach, Raymond Domenech, who was something of a silent assassin during his playing days with St Etienne and Lyon, was not too upset with what he had seen. Lyon directeur sportif Bernard Lacombe, club secretary Marino Faccioli, and president Jean Michel Aulas were a little perplexed by it all. Sometime later, after I did sign for Lyon, Peter told me that they wanted to know why the club were interested in a madman like me! Having thought I had blown my chances I heard then that they were going to come back and have another look at me. They would have to wait for the Cup semi-final against Hibs because, once again, I found myself suspended.

ARE YOU SURE, REF? – I'm just about to be sent off against Hearts in a Scottish Cup quarter-final clash in March 1989 – and the representatives from Olympique Lyon are up in the stand watching me!

MY BEST CELTIC GAME

Hampden Park was the venue for the semi-final and it was to turn out to be one of my best games ever in a Celtic shirt. Hibs had signed Coventry City's big centre forward Keith Houchen during the previous season and they were expecting him to do the damage against us. He had played in the Cup final the year before at Wembley and scored a great goal as Coventry surprised the much-fancied Tottenham 3-2. But I was on my game, Keith wasn't getting a look in and after ten minutes I went up for a corner kick and bulleted the ball into the back of the Hibs' net. Ten minutes into the game, 1-0 up, and I'm playing out of my skin. And sitting somewhere up there in the stand were the representatives from Lyon. Great. Now we were in the final and it felt great coming off the pitch that day. Celtic gave me permission to speak to Lyon and after having a quick beer with the team I went up to the director's room to meet them. It was here that I met Peter for the first time. He was interpreting for everybody, but they all looked a little sheepish when I started on about my goal, rare as they are for me. Then Peter told me. Traffic had delayed them on the way in from the airport and they arrived after twelve minutes of the game – two minutes after I had scored!

1989 SCOTTISH CUP FINAL

But we got negotiations rolling and a move was on the cards at the end of the season. First, however, came the small matter of the Scottish Cup final – against Rangers. Our traditional foes had won everything so far, the Skol Cup, the League Championship, and their fans were walking around the streets of Glasgow wearing treble-champion tee-shirts – and we hadn't even met in the Scottish Cup final yet!

Ironically we were all quite laid back about the whole thing. I don't think we were as nervous as before the semi-final. If you fall at that fence there is nothing left. Now we had a chance to put one over on Rangers. And when we walked out onto the pitch, the noise, the atmosphere was great. The first forty-five minutes were quite un-eventful. Then Roy Aitken, probably the most experienced player on the field, took a quick throw-in which caught the Rangers off guard. They were still arguing about whose ball it was, but the referee was having none of it. The ball was swept up-field and then their right fullback, Gary Stevens, made a complete hash of a back pass and Joe Miller was on it like a flash to send it crashing into the back of the Rangers net.

They came back at us almost from the kick-off but we managed to clear our lines. As the match progressed they began to get ruffled and threw everything at us, and it appeared to pay off when Terry Butcher was told to move up-field to add extra height to their attack as they began to bombard us. They had the ball in the net at one stage but the referee ruled it out because Packie Bonner had been fouled by Davie

CHAMPIONS! Here we are with the Scottish FA Cup after beating Dundee United in May 1988. Can you spot my Irish teammates Packie Bonner and Chris Morris? Answers on the back of a tenner, please.

Cooper. They came forward in droves, kept up the pressure, and then, once again, Roy Aitken took the fight out of them. With just a couple of minutes left and our penalty area under siege, we got a free kick right at the corner flag. Roy got Joe Miller to roll the ball to him. We all thought he was going to keep it down at the corner flag or boot it up-field to waste some more time – but not Roy. No, he flicked it up and volleyed it as hard and as far as he could into the Rangers fans behind their goal!

By the time the fans gave the ball back there was about a minute left and we soon ran out the clock to win the Cup. What a way to finish my career with Celtic. I've enjoyed my career at every club I've played for, but Celtic was something special because of the success that I was a part of. There was also a great spirit amongst the players, a great feeling of camaraderie. There were some real characters, like Roy Aitken who had been with the club for years and was a big part

DOUBLE TAKE – Ladies and gentlemen, it's Mick McCarthy – and Mick McCarthy. This is Michael on one of his first visits to Celtic Park.

of Celtic when I was there, Mark McGhee, the team's practical joker, Tommy Burns, another player steeped in the Celtic tradition, and then there were the hit men, Peter Grant and Paul McStay.

Nobody could understand my relationship with Peter Grant. We argued at training sessions, argued so much that we almost came to blows most of the time. We chased each other around the training pitch just to tackle each other. But that was because we were so much alike – a pair of lads who have this hard exterior but are actually a pair of softies. We roomed together when we travelled and were the best of mates. But everybody at Celtic played their part in making the club what it was.

LYON

THE ONE THING THAT THREW A SHADOW over my move to Lyon was a nagging injury I had carried for the second half of the season with Celtic. My right knee was causing me considerable pain after games and it was getting worse. So that summer, after much soul-searching and advice from my old teacher Norman Rimmington at Barnsley, I had an operation. I talked to Peter Boyle on the telephone and asked them if Lyon were still interested. He said Yes, so I went over to sign for them – and walked off the plane with my leg all bandaged up and limping! They had planned to wire me, do tests, put me on an exercise bike, but they couldn't. Yet they still wanted me and after a little haggling, even though I had my leg all strapped up, I signed for Olympique Lyon.

MY FAMILY

There had been some sleepless nights too before I finally put pen to paper and signed for Lyon. The contract was good and it would last for three years yet I was worried about the kids. They had been born in Manchester and had begun to grow up in Glasgow. Indeed the girls and even little Michael had already developed a slight Scottish accent. But the move was just as much for them and Fiona. The three-year contract was very good and would help me put some money aside for our future. I shouldn't have worried too much about the children. They took to Lyons like ducks to water. But they do have to be thought about. When we were leaving Glasgow there were a few little tears because they were leaving their friends. It can be hard on them because they move around a lot. You get them settled somewhere and then you could be on the move again very soon.

They are still too young for me to explain to them that what I do is all for them and the future. I make as much time as I can to spend with them. The kids and Fiona are my whole life. And even though I spend quite a lot of time away from home because of my profession, I probably spend more time with them than a lot of parents do with their children. When I was a youngster growing up in Barnsley my father worked a twelve-hour shift, six to six every day. I might come in at eight in the evening and he'd be there and I'd say 'Hello Dad'; he'd say 'Hello Mick', and then I'd be off upstairs to get ready to go out again!

We moved into a house in Dardilly, an idyllic little village about seven or eight miles from the centre of Lyons. Peter Boyle lived close by and that made it so much easier for us because he could speak French. There wasn't too much of a culture shock either. When you're a football player you tend to live away from the club and normally in an affluent area, so you're cossetted from the problems that every big city has. Anyway, professionals tend to be protected from the real world. I know football is still a working class game, but although you go and meet the fans at presentations in pubs and clubs you don't go home with them.

LANGUAGE PROBLEMS

We were there only a week and already the kids were picking up the language. I found it somewhat harder to master and that, I would say, was my main problem during my stay. It's so important to make an effort and learn the language of a country you intend to stay in for a while. I remember on my first day training with the club I was trying my hardest and when things didn't go right I'd say, 'F...k it!' The directeur sportif, Bernard Lacombe, heard me and called Peter Boyle over. He wanted to know why I kept saying that. What did it mean? Peter spent a long time explaining that one away.

Language problems aside, everything else was going well for my family. Anna and Katie had enrolled into a wonderful school not far from our new home. They loved it and Fiona and I were very happy with it too. The girls went off at around half-past eight in the morning, came home for lunch and went back to school until around five in the evening – SIX days a week! Our neighbours were very friendly as well, which knocked the myth that French people were cold and unfriendly. Some, admittedly, were a little aloof, but over a period of time we all became firm friends. Even now if I go back for a visit they will be out to meet and greet me even though I spent less than a year there.

The first day I arrived for training the only French words I knew were the usual ones that any dumbo learns – *bonjour, au revoir, merci*, that kind of thing. So I hopped on the club coach for an eight-hour journey to our training camp in Germany and nobody on the bus spoke English except me. Great!

INJURIES

I didn't train while in Germany. The club were very understanding about the knee injury. When we returned to Lyons the club got me through pre-season workouts and got me fit for their first match against Marseilles. It was also Chris Waddle's debut since his £4.5 million transfer from Tottenham to Marseilles. Lyon played me as a sweeper, a position I was not used to and we were well beaten 4-1. I got my first write-up in French with a headline over it that said it all: *'Debut Catastrophique'*. That summed it up very well.

I settled then well enough and stayed in the team for the next ten games, until my knee acted up again. The club were great. They could have 'solved' the problem by injecting the knee on a regular basis, but they refused to do that. Instead their physiotherapist George Halatas put me on a series of exercises to help the knee mend. The physio was brilliant. I had never come across one in Britain who knew so much about his profession.

Before the injury I had begun to make an impression on the rest of my teammates and fans, and coach Raymond Domenech loved it all. He felt that the team needed a little British steel and I was brought in to do the job. I was enjoying my stay in Lyon except for the injury. And still the club were great to me. If I had to have time off for the knee to heal, then that's what would happen. There would be no jabs. I would get better, the club said, and then I could play out my contract with them. They were so good to me, at times I felt embarrassed.

1990 SEASON

At the beginning of the new year I felt as fit as a flea. I played in a few friendlies and felt great. I thought I was ready to make my comeback but Raymond left me out. I couldn't blame him. The team had played well at the end of the first part of the season and they deserved a chance to continue without any changes. Needless to say I wasn't too happy. But Raymond was proved right when the club went from strength to strength and climbed the table. So I was in the reserves playing away and Raymond would come and watch me. He was pleased with my attitude and he told me that not many first-team players would treat a spell in the reserves as professionally as I did. That was nice of him, but I still wasn't getting back into the first team.

I had another problem now. The World Cup was looming on the horizon. This was January 1990, Ireland had qualified, and in just a few short months we would be off to Italy for the finals. I thought Jack Charlton would probably take me no matter what happened – but I didn't want to go to Italy for the ride. I wanted to play. I had to start playing again, and if that meant a move then so be it. I didn't want to leave Lyons. I was enjoying it too much and the family loved it. After a few tentative steps when I arrived, I had been accepted by my teammates and the fans. Indeed, even the referees, for a change, took to me!

In one particular match, against Montpellier, it was getting a little physical. Now 'physical' on the Continent is a little bit different than at home. They commit more fouls off the ball when the referee is not watching – pulling your hair, pinching you, things like that. Anyway, the ball was knocked towards our goal and I could see that three of them were heading for it. Their aim was to get the ball and me. But I just thundered in and smacked the ball away, and they went up in the air with it! I just looked at the referee and knew it was time for an early bath. I walked off without saying a word. I was sick that I had been sent off but there was no point in arguing.

Just after the match ended the president came into the dressingroom and he looked happy! I'd been sent off and he was happy! But then he explained that the referee could not believe my conduct. French players will run up to the referee and argue with him until the cows come home when they're sent off. The coach normally has to come onto the pitch and pull the offender off. But this referee wrote a glowing report about my dignified behaviour and I only got a one-match ban!

Around late February or early March, Millwall approached Lyon about taking me on loan until the end of the season. They were struggling at the foot of Division One and their manager John Docherty had been sacked. Bob Pearson had been appointed as caretaker and telephoned Lyon.

LAST DAYS AT LYON

The move was one I needed – to be playing regular first-team football to make sure I was match fit. I needed to have some games under my belt. I went over to London with the Lyon secretary Marino Faccioli and the directeur sportif Bernard Lacombe. I'll never forget the drive from Heathrow to the Millwall grounds, The Den, in Cold Blow Lane in southeast London. It was grey, raining and the journey seemed to last forever. As Marino and Bernard looked out the window of the cab they scratched their heads and wondered why I wanted to leave a beautiful place like Lyons – a great set-up, wonderful stadium and a brilliant lifestyle for this!

But Bob Pearson and Graham Horthorp, the club secretary, put me at ease straight away. The surroundings might not have been much to look at but the club was a very homely one. It reminded me of Barnsley. The lad making tea and sandwiches, and the girls in the office – they were all very friendly. It was all 'Hello, how are you doing?' Polite and sincere. It was extraordinary really. I was back at a club where I could talk to people. There was no language barrier. We yapped about everything, family, weather, music, houses, and even football. They couldn't stop me talking. I made up my mind to come home.

I learned a tremendous amount at Lyon even though I didn't play that many games. Their approach to playing the game was obviously different to the British game but off the field there are also many differences to what I was used to back home. For a start the players are, generally, much more disciplined and professional. They look after their bodies, eating the right food and drinking very little alcohol at any time of the year. They train hard, twice a day, and then go home to their families. There is no such thing as all the lads going off for a few beers. It was very rare to see any of them drink anything stronger than fruit juice. Their whole approach was great. Players were looked after very well by the club. No expense was spared when injuries had to be treated. There was no rushing players back to play if they were almost fit. The players respected that and it made them more determined to play well for the club.

If I have one criticism of the French game, and the Continental game generally, then it's the fannying about players get up to out on the field when they're supposedly injured. Some lads I played against would scream blue murder and roll around on the ground in front of the referee if you even said *bonjour* to them. I don't like a professional player trying to get another one sent off. Many times I ran up to a player who was lying there giving an Oscar-winning performance on the deck and lifted him and told him, in no uncertain terms, what I thought of him.

BACK IN ENGLAND

I walked into a club which seemed to be in turmoil at Millwall. Like all clubs who face relegation, nothing seemed to go right. The rot had actually set in at the end of the previous season. The club had made it into the First Division for the first time and had an exceptional start but then tended to live on that when they hit a bad patch after Christmas. The rot wasn't stopped at the beginning of the 1989/90 season and so the problem arose. Bob Pearson had been thrown in at the deep end when John Docherty went, and it would have been a miracle if he had managed to rescue the club from the drop.

The players did try, but I think if Bob could have signed the whole of the West German World Cup winning team it wouldn't have made a difference. There was an air of inevitability at The Den. We were doomed and that was that. I knew that Bob was in trouble too when he called me aside one day and told me that no matter what happened he would be making a recommendation to the club that they sign me permanently. Little did I know, in those final few weeks of the season, that Bruce Rioch was watching our games. Then the board announced that he had been confirmed as manager. Soon afterwards, Bruce called me in and told me that he wanted me to stay.

Bruce, a fine midfield player who had a distinguished career with clubs like Derby and Everton and with Scotland, had done a marvellous job at Middlesbrough, taking the club from being close to extinction to Division One. He's a strict disciplinarian, which is fine by me, with a great backroom staff including my old Barnsley mate Ian Evans, the new England assistant Steve Harrison (the greatest cabaret act in the Football League) and Ian McNeill as assistant manager. Now Millwall are fighting to get back into the First Division and with a little luck they could well be back there next season. I have no regrets about joining Millwall, and I hope I can be part of the success which will come to the club in the near future.

EURO '88

EUROPEAN CHAMPIONSHIP QUALIFIERS

BELGIUM (BRUSSELS)

IRELAND'S PATH TO THE 1988 EUROPEAN CHAMPIONSHIP finals in West Germany had four obstructions – Bulgaria, Belgium, Scotland and Luxembourg. Some looked tougher than others. But in the end they were all hard games, including the two fixtures against Luxembourg. But Jack Charlton had prepared the squad. We had got to know each other and there was an air of confidence within the squad that we could qualify for the final stages of the Championships.

Injury ruled me out of the first match, a clash with Belgium in Brussels on Wednesday, September 10, 1986. I'd just had an exploratory operation on my knee in Manchester. I remember driving home that night, trying to tune into the game on RTE radio. The reception, however, was terrible and it was only later that I found out we had drawn with the Belgians 2-2, Frank Stapleton and Liam Brady scoring the all-important goals.

I talked to Frank sometime later about that match. It was significant for other reasons. That particular match was the first to be played in the Heysel stadium after the horror of the disaster there during the Liverpool-Juventus European Champions' Cup final when thirty-eight Italian fans had been killed. Included in the Liverpool team that evening in May 1986 were Mark Lawrenson and Ronnie Whelan. Mark played for the Republic against Belgium and Ronnie came on as a substitute. Our match against the Belgians must have rekindled that nightmare for them.

The Belgian authorities were also worried that the 'British' fans who travelled to the match might cause problems. Brussels was still recovering from the Heysel disaster and any disturbances at the match against Belgium that night would, I'm sure, have been squashed with an iron fist. But the Belgians needn't have worried. Our fans were not 'British'. They were Irish and they behaved themselves with all the dignity that would earn them respect all around Europe in the coming years.

SCOTLAND (DUBLIN)

The following month we were back in Dublin preparing for the visit of Scotland. The game ended 0-0, a pretty nondescript match. We had them on the rack for most of the game. We battered them for ninety minutes, but just couldn't score. It wasn't a great game and although we were happy to get a point we should really have wrapped it up and taken them.

Still, we were unbeaten so far. We had two points and we felt that if we could keep the same squad together we could qualify for the finals. Yet the nature of the competition meant that we hadn't got another match in the Championships until February 1987, a whole four months away. However, Jack pulled us back together the following month for a friendly against Poland in Warsaw. We lost that one 1-0 on November 12, but the main exercise was to get the lads back together again, keep the spirit, get us working as a team. So, although we were beaten, the trip did have its up-side.

SCOTLAND (GLASGOW)

We met up three days before the return tie against Scotland on Sunday, February 15, in Glasgow. We had a night out on Sunday, had a few beers and caught up on all the gossip. Although some of us had run into each other on the pitch when our clubs met in the Football League, I hadn't seen all the players so there was a lot to talk about. We were very relaxed for the match against the Scots at Hampden Park the following Wednesday night.

It was an unusual team selection. Jack played Paul McGrath and Ronnie Whelan in the fullback slots, Kevin Moran and myself at the centre of defence, Ray Houghton, Liam Brady and Mark Lawrenson in midfield and Frank Stapleton, Tony Galvin and John Aldridge up-front. I can remember thinking as we went out how big and physical our back line was – and Scotland were playing Mo Johnston, Pat Nevin and Brian McClair in their attack. They played right into

Jack's hands. They were going with three lightweight, talented front-runners against our back four. They were never going to match us physically – and they didn't.

Obviously the Scottish fans knew what was on the cards because they stayed away in droves. The game was probably the turning point for the Irish team. We went ahead, John Aldridge rolled the ball to Lawro from a free kick and he had it in the back of the net before the Scottish defence knew what was happening. Mark would play only two further games for the Republic before injury ended his career. He was a great loss to us. There he was, probably the best centre-half in Europe playing for his country in midfield and scoring the winner. Mark could play anywhere, he was so talented. He was the complete player, good in the air, fast on the ground, a great footballing brain and a player capable of taking on and beating players. Even now Liverpool have found it hard to replace him. By this time even our critics were beginning to sit up. We had four points from three games, two of them away from home. Ireland was on the march.

BULGARIA (SOFIA)

The next qualifying game, Bulgaria in Sofia, was always going to be a tough one. This was, remember, pre-Perestroika days in Eastern Europe, and games behind the Iron Curtain had always been tough affairs. The referees were often intimidated. We were beaten 2-1, we should have got at least a point. Frank Stapleton kept us in the game with a fine goal. But they edged a torrid encounter with a penalty.

I was blamed for their first goal. My critics say I was slow getting to the ball against Cirikov. But the video shows clearly what happened. I actually beat him to the ball and was preparing to clear our lines when he pushed me, with both hands, in the back. It was so blatant, he almost bowled me over before crossing for Sadkov to score. I was so disappointed after that game. I felt cheated too. I don't ever like losing, but when you've been cheated as well it makes it so much worse. I felt very low, I thought I had let the rest of the lads down. But they were great and rallied around me. I was determined that when we met in Dublin we would take them apart and Cirikov wouldn't get a look in. Maybe I should have taken a little more heed of the date we had played them – April Fool's Day! I was determined Cirikov would be the fool when we met in Dublin later that year.

BELGIUM (DUBLIN)

Just four short weeks later we were back at Lansdowne for our return clash with Belgium on April 29, 1987. On the day we had played Bulgaria in Sofia, Belgium had taken Scotland apart in Brussels 4-1, with Nico Claesen scoring three. All the talk in the newspapers prior to the match was Claesen, Claesen, Claesen – what he was going to do to us, how he was going to take Kevin Moran and myself apart at the back.

On the day, he didn't get a look in. Belgium played him up-front by himself and played everybody in deep positions. They had come for a point. We bombarded their goalmouth all afternoon. We played well – but again we should have come away with two points instead of a single one after a 0-0 draw.

LUXEMBOURG (AWAY)

When we played Luxembourg away, on May 27, 1987, I had moved from Manchester City to Glasgow Celtic eight days earlier and I was just feeling my way around my new club. It was a game we had to win. We knew it was going to be difficult because when you come up against one of the really smaller nations you're expected to slaughter them. But it doesn't always work that way. You have to motivate yourself that little bit more and must always remember that they have nothing to lose. They are expected to be beaten, they have no worries. But if you're beaten then it's big news. There were only 4,290 people at that match – a fair percentage of them Irish – and we duly beat them 2-0, with goals from Tony Galvin and Ronnie Whelan.

John Aldridge finally broke his Irish duck with a 'goal' in the second half of this match. Aldo had been one of the most prolific scorers in the English League with Newport County, Oxford, and, at that time, Liverpool. He was worth twenty goals a season. But in the Irish set-up he played a different game and had yet to score. So John pops the ball in the back of the net and he's off up the pitch to celebrate. Arms in the air and running towards the fans who were so happy for him. Then the referee blows for off-side and disallows Aldo's goal. He almost went spare and was duly booked. We all had a good laugh after at his expense but also felt sorry for him. He was trying so hard for Ireland and doing a great job by distracting opponents who knew about his prolific goalscoring record.

LUXEMBOURG (DUBLIN)

In September we had the return match against Luxembourg in Dublin. I missed it through injury. But the lads told me we struggled. Indeed, they scored first through Krings, and for a while it looked like they might grab an historic away victory. But the Irish team were never going to let that happen. They didn't want to be the first European team to fall to Luxembourg. Goals from Frank again and Paul McGrath made sure we collected the points.

BULGARIA (DUBLIN)

To have any chance to qualify for the finals in Germany we had to beat the Bulgarians at Lansdowne the following month. The players were keyed up for this one. We all felt we had been robbed in Sofia the previous April. I was also desperate to see my mate Cirikov again. I had a niggling injury, but I would have gone out onto the pitch that day on a crutch just to 'greet' him. I still hadn't got over the way he had pushed me in Sofia. But there was more to it than that. He had spat on my face out there, and had done the same, disgraceful thing to Kevin Moran as we walked off the pitch at the END of the game. If anyone had annoyed me in football he had.

I had a good game that day. I swore to myself before the match that he wasn't going to get the better of me. I was only on the pitch and he started. He was mouthing to me, even told me to 'F...k off' – most foreign players know those two English words. I was marking him and the game was getting physical because we began to inflict our game on them. Then there was a bit of a ruck, one of their lads had thrown in a bad tackle on Ronnie Whelan. It looked like it was going to get ugly so I went and grabbed my mate Cirikov and pulled him away. I would have loved to put some manners on him there and then but I knew that was what he wanted – me to lose my temper and then the referee would give me my marching orders. When he saw I wasn't going to take the bait he just walked up to me, looked me straight in the eye and spat all over my face. I looked back at him, and just laughed. He went spare. He couldn't believe my reaction – neither could I – and for the rest of the match he never got a real kick of the ball. Paul McGrath and Kevin Moran scored and we won handsomely 2-0. However, Liam Brady was sent off. They kicked lumps out of Liam all afternoon and after another terrible tackle Liam retaliated and was shown the red card.

We had finished our group matches and had eleven points having lost just one game. But the Bulgarians, then on ten points, still had one game to play, against Scotland in Bulgaria. It didn't look too good for us. That match was scheduled for Wednesday, November 11. The night before, we played a friendly match in Dublin at Dalymount Park against Israel and hammered them 5-0. It was David Kelly's debut for the Republic and he marked it with a hat-trick. It was also the night that my new Celtic teammate Chris Morris made his debut.

I stayed to watch the Bulgarian game on TV, I sat watching with Johnny Giles. All the Bulgarians needed was a draw and they were through. At half-time it was scoreless and Scotland never looked like scoring. With ten minutes to go, however, Gordon Durie swung the ball across the Bulgarian goalmouth, Hearts' Gary McKay was there to meet it and bang! – the Scots are in front.

The Bulgarians didn't know what hit them. They swept up the field and laid siege to the Scottish goal, but they just couldn't score. The Bulgarians were beaten – and we were on our way to Germany the following summer for the European Championship finals.

Then the jibes began. We had got to the finals thanks to Scotland. Nonsense. Getting to Germany was based on results over eight matches and we had the best results. Anyway, I didn't care how we got there – front door, back door or through a window, we were going! Unfortunately that red card against the Bulgarians was to prove a nightmare for Liam Brady. He got a four-match ban which was reduced to two on appeal. Liam was destined to sit out the finals in Germany.

THE EUROPEAN CHAMPIONSHIPS

THE EUROPEAN CHAMPIONSHIP FINALS in West Germany were actually a bonus for Jack. He had been building the team, trying out new players and generally getting the team in order for the 1990 World Cup qualifying tournament. But we were going to Germany and everybody from Jack down was taking it all deadly seriously.

I played in three friendly matches before we went to the finals – all good warm-up games against the kind of opposition and style of play Jack thought we might face in Germany. In March 1988 we beat Romania at Lansdowne. We won 2-0. It could have been a lot more. There was confidence in the team now. Jack had got us believing in ourselves, believing that we could take on anybody and either beat them or give them a bloody good game. That result was a big lift and when we took on the Yugoslavians the following month, and beat them by two goals as well, our confidence began to run sky-high.

I remember that game for two reasons: it was Mark Kelly's debut – the Slavs tried to kick the young winger off the pitch but he had a fabulous match; and I scored my first goal for Ireland. It was a corner, I went up at the near post and headed it home. I knew I had put it away – but then John Sheridan claimed that the ball had gone into the net direct from his corner. I wasn't particularly bothered once we won – but then the boys from RTE came down after the match and told the lads that I had definitely got a touch to it.

By now we knew who we would be playing in Germany. We were in Group Two, along with England, the USSR and Holland. We were regarded as the make-weights in the group. The squad was staying at Finnstown House just outside Lucan, County Dublin. We had gathered there towards the end of May. We trained every day and then just relaxed. When we weren't training Jack arranged all kinds of things for the lads. He took them to the races one day. I didn't go as I was resting. They had a great day and on the way back they began to sing 'One Jackie Charlton, there's only one Jackie Charlton … Beer, beer we want more beer.' So Jack said right, and the coach stopped at the next pub. And all the way back they stopped at *every* pub and had a drink!

The following day we were training again and by now we have a routine – warm-up exercise, a little running and then a little five-a-side knockabout. Jack loves to keep the goalkeepers on their toes in the warm-up, so Gerry Peyton and Packie Bonner are in between the posts and Jack is knocking hell out of balls at them. Little Charlie O'Leary, the equipment officer, has a part in this too. Charlie has to roll the ball for Jack to strike. Jack is kicking in his training shoes and he pulls a calf muscle. Poor old Charlie gets the blame of course. 'Why did you roll that ball to me like that, now I've gone and done my calf muscle in,' Jack shouts at Charlie. We all laugh. Charlie gets the blame for everything.

Tuesday, we're out on the training pitch again. We have completed all our warm-ups and it's time for the five-a-side. Because of Jack's pulled muscle, Maurice Setters, his assistant, is overseeing training. We're playing this great game of keep-ball. The lads are sharp and if you haven't got the ball you're running your nuts off to get it back. It's probably the best game of keep-ball I have ever played. Then Jack sees what we are at and comes down. 'Stop it, stop that straight away,' he's shouting as he hobbles over. So we stop. We just don't know what's going on. 'I told you we don't play keep-ball,' Jack screams. 'We don't pass it about, because if you do it training, we'll start passing it about in games!' Everything stopped, stone dead. I know what Jack meant, but it was strange at the time – and very funny. The match against Norway was played the following night, Wednesday, June 1. It was a nothing game. Nobody wanted to get injured so we played it cautiously and it ended up 0-0. We hadn't been beaten and nobody got hurt. We had a couple more days training in Norway before heading off to West Germany and Euro'88.

ENGLAND

There was a tremendous buzz in the squad. The Republic of Ireland had never been to major finals before. We were all looking forward to it. We were like a pub team heading off for their first ever trip abroad, or a bunch of schoolkids. As soon as we touched down in Stuttgart the security was tremendous. We were whisked off to our hotel along with what seemed like a coachload of reporters. There was intense interest in us back home, obviously from the Irish media, but also from the British media because our first match was against England. We had some novelty value for them. But as far as they were concerned we were just there to make up the numbers in Group Two.

Jack was great with the press. He handled them magnificently, did most of the interviews. The senior members of the squad were also wanted for interviews, people like Frank Stapleton and Liam Brady (who came along to advise even though he wasn't in the squad).

Our training sessions shocked the media. The first morning, Friday, June 10, set the scene for the rest of the trip. I was still suffering a little with my knee and had a jog around the training ground. Another couple of the lads were doing press-ups, somebody else was having a run round on his own and Jack would be taking those who were fit for a light workout. The rest of the sick, lame and lazy basically did what they wanted and had a jog with Mick Byrne, the physio. Then there would be a little shooting practice – crossing to the keepers, headers. I remember Trevor Brooking, the former England and West Ham midfielder coming to watch us. He stood scratching his head.

We'd end every training session with one of those five-a-sides and Jack would stop them abruptly: 'Right, that's it. Come on let's go, you've done enough,' he'd shout, and we'd be off. That's all we did. But on Saturday, not long before we set off for the stadium in Stuttgart to have a run out on the pitch, my legs seemed to seize up. I was playing cards with some of the lads and when I stood up this pain shot through my calves. They seemed to lock up. They appeared to be hard – you could knock on them just like a door. Mick Byrne said: 'Don't worry. They'll be all right by the time we get to the training ground.' But when we got there I could barely walk. The calves were rock solid. It's been put down to the manic bus journey to the ground, to nervous tension, put down to all sorts of things, but to this day I still don't know what it was.

Now I was worried. My chances of playing against England appeared to be on the way out the window. If it wasn't for Mick Byrne I wouldn't have played. He got me back at the hotel, socks down and filled them with ice and he mollycoddled me. 'If you're not playing there'll be trouble. We've got to have the same team out that's done us proud,' Mick kept saying to me. He really worked on me, on my back, ice treatment, rubbed my legs, used anti-inflammatories. All this, and I'm still saying 'I've no chance of playing, I've no f...king chance.' But Mick wasn't giving up. There was treatment all night before I went to bed but I still kept telling him that I was struggling.

The following morning I was up early for a fitness test. Mick gave me a good rub. The calves were a little easier now, but still sore. He strapped me up very tightly and I went for a run with Paul McGrath, who had taken a knock in training, and Packie, who was having problems with his back. There were cameras from British TV there and they wanted to know what was going on, but nobody was telling them anything. As I ran I began to think that I might be able to play. I wanted to play so badly – so I told Mick that I was okay. But I would have to play with these enormous strappings under my socks. If I had taken them off I knew that my calves would just seize up.

Back at breakfast that morning you could feel the tension beginning to build up. Most of the lads were surprisingly quiet. Then Jack walked in and he spotted John Aldridge. 'Ah, just the man I want to see,' Jack said so everybody could hear him. 'Now listen, John, you haven't scored a goal for Ireland yet, so don't go breaking the habit of a lifetime this afternoon against England. I want to be out of here next Sunday, I've got a fishing trip booked for the following week and I don't want to be stuck here in Germany for some bloody European Championship final!' It was astonishing what he said that morning. But it worked. We all burst into laughter and the tension had been broken. We knew there was no way that Jack would mean something like that. He wanted to win just as much as we did.

In the dressingroom before the game Jack kept up his confident air. He kept talking like that all the time – we should be out of here next weekend, really looking forward to that fishing trip. Let's get these three games over and piss off home! He was playing the England match down as much as he could. It had been built up so much by the media and of course it was Us versus Them, the old enemy. And it was important to the lads, this was *the* game we didn't want to lose. Jack tried to defuse that a little and what he was basically trying to say was: 'Whatever happens, we've still got another two games to play, we don't want to get beaten by them, but even if we do, we've two more games to play and we can still go through to the semi-finals.'

That was the theme of it. Jack went around trying to relax everybody, had a word with us all. He wasn't building the game up, he wasn't talking about any one individual player and saying Oh he's playing well and he could cause us problems. He just said: 'If you do this and you do that, we stick to our pattern of play, inflict our pattern on them, then we can beat them.' He was so confident and he put it over so well, that we went out knowing we *could* beat them. And Jack was fooling them all. Johann Cruyff said it at the World Cup, Jack conned everybody, and I think he did it there, in Germany, playing the country bumpkin bit, like we were there for the ride, we were lucky to get here and we were going to enjoy ourselves – and all the time he was putting the pressure on to England.

And it worked. We didn't play that well and yet we beat them. They just couldn't pull Ray Houghton's early goal back. We did everything Jack told us – brilliantly – and came away with a 1-0 victory. Gary Lineker missed a dozen chances, the kind that he wouldn't miss in another month of Sundays.

And of course after the game ended the excuses began. So Gary Lineker did have hepatitis as the British press said, but then my calves were banjaxed and we weren't making a big thing about that. Big Packie was to have a tremendous tournament with a bad back injury, an injury that required surgery soon after the Championships, but we never used that as an excuse when we finally went out of the competition. After the post-match interviews there was time for a beer at the stadium and time to reflect on what had happened. Already our fans were celebrating in the streets of Stuttgart. I was told later it was bedlam back in Ireland, and we were going to have a good night as well. A lot of people thought it was a one-off. And others said: 'Well, that's your Championships, you've beaten England now you can pack up and go home.' No way. We had two points and just two more would put us through to the semi-finals.

Now the lads were knocking back the beers at the stadium and Jack said, 'Right, onto the bus and back to the hotel.' But when we got onto the coach we couldn't find Tony Galvin. Then the word gets back to us that Tony is still being dope-tested. Two players are picked randomly after each match to give a urine sample. Tony had been picked – but he was finding it hard to give a sample. So it was back into the stadium for a few more beers. It was all for one and one for all, we weren't leaving Tony behind. That was the kind of collective- ness that was growing within the squad. So we were back upstairs and the sing-song starts in the stadium bar – and there was one going on outside with the fans too.

Finally Tony arrived, took a right pasting from the lads, and we were off to our hotel. We had beaten England and we wanted to celebrate, so Jack said, 'Okay, once you're in bed by midnight.' Jack had set a curfew. Some of the lads had never had one, others thought a curfew was a small flightless bird with a long beak! It was a great night at the hotel, just great crack. And then just before midnight Jack came around with Mick Byrne and made sure we headed for bed. We had an early start the following morning.

USSR

I was beginning to wonder if there were only very early-morning flights when the Irish team travelled! We always seemed to be up early and on a plane heading for the next venue. We stayed at a sports complex in Hanover. The rooms were basic, nice but basic – bed, sink, bath, shower. The sporting facilities were wonderful but everything else was a little sparse. The lads had a moan about their rooms. No tea-making facilities? No stationery? As if anyone was going to sit down and write a letter.

Out on the training ground we kept losing balls. The place was surrounded by trees and we kept hitting balls into them. We had arrived in Hanover early on Monday, June 13, and we were due to meet the Soviets on Wednesday evening. Training was the usual and then there were the media interviews. They loved us in Germany. We were available all the time. You might get a telephone call in your room from a reporter and then you were back downstairs for another interview.

Thankfully, we were due to play the Soviets in the evening. Our match against England had been an afternoon kick-off in blistering heat. It had drained us. We were into a routine now, training, inter- views, eat, sleep and then there was our little room at all the hotels which was sacrosanct. We went in there to get away from everything. It was a room where only the players and Jack, Maurice Setters, Mick

Byrne, Charlie O'Leary and maybe one or two other members of the party were allowed to go.

On Tuesday night we went to have a look at the stadium, had a little knockabout, and then it was back to our sports complex. We weren't worried about the Soviets at all. We knew they were a good team but we also knew that it would be cooler because of the evening kick-off and that we would be in a better position to inflict our game on them.

As we sat in the dressingroom before the game Jack went through his routine. 'Close them down; put them under pressure; inflict our game on them; don't let them dictate things.' We were now top of Group Two with the Soviet Union because they had beaten Holland in their first match. So a victory against them would put us into the European Championship semi-finals.

We were all over the Soviets that night. For the first forty-five minutes they never got a look in, and of course Ronnie Whelan scored that wonderful goal with a brilliant volley – the goal of the tournament. We were made up when we came in at half-time. We had them on the rack.

In the second half we should have had a penalty when Tony Galvin was fouled in their penalty area. I have watched it on video since and it was a definite penalty. Aldo had a couple of chances too – but we were coasting into the semi-finals. Then with six minutes left, they struck and nicked a goal back. And as soon as they did, they shut up shop, they pulled everybody back behind the ball. They held on for a draw, 1-1. I had never seen a team so sick and dejected. We were, without doubt, the better team and ended up with just one point. That reaction showed the growing maturity and confidence in the team – we had drawn with the powerful Soviets on foreign soil and we were disappointed. A few short years ago that would have been greeted as something of a milestone.

Now the Soviets and ourselves had three points each and that afternoon the Dutch had mauled England 3-1. England, who had come to the tournament as one of the favourites, were bottom of our group with no points. And Ireland, who had come as fodder for the other nations, were just one point away from a semi-final place. The Dutch had to beat us to qualify.

That evening back at our headquarters we sit up going back over the game. Jack is delighted we've got a result. But he's on a bit of a downer as well. We played so well we could have won. But then he's beginning to lift us for the match against the Dutch on Saturday. 'Come on, we've got to play Holland, you've proved that you can do it. We're going to beat Holland, you know,' Jack says. 'They're no better than us. Russia beat Holland, I know that doesn't mean we'll beat them, but the point is we've nothing to worry about playing Holland.' In another breath Jack is saying: 'If you get a point, we go through – and that's me fishing trip off.' He's still on that theme. He is still Mr Joviality Himself.

HOLLAND

The same again the following morning, Thursday, June 16. Up early and off to Gelsenkirchen. Our home-from-home there was in a place that looked like a converted fifteenth-century farmhouse. The ceilings were so low that a lot of us were walking around ducking our heads. Packie, in particular, was suffering. He was bent over most of the time.

We weren't there too long when someone found out that the swimming pool was a haven for nudists. So the lads are making themselves busy – they want to have a look. But Jack pulls us aside and tells us that there's a photographer on the prowl. 'He'll be looking for some dirt on us,' Jack warned. So the swimming was immediately put out of bounds. We had a good record up to then and we knew that at some time or another some of the tackier newspapers would be nosing around looking for some scandal. There was no way we were going to do their job for them. That was the first really serious chat we had with Jack, and he was right. We didn't want any garbage in the papers about ourselves.

By now most of the British press have deserted the English camp and moved in with us. The hotel is packed and the hype for the Dutch match is starting to build up. But Jack made sure it wouldn't get to us. He handled the press really well, gave them enough to talk about without giving anything away. We trained and just fooled around on Thursday and Friday.

The only worry for the match was Packie. On Friday morning he came down and he wasn't the best. Packie is such a likeable big man, he's a gentleman, he hasn't got a bit of nastiness in him – but he's never great in the morning, and on this particular morning he was grumpier than ever. He was suffering with his back. I said, 'Good morning, Packie.' He just growled at me and I knew he wasn't feeling the best. He went for a fitness test and when he came back in Jack said, 'That's it, Packie is fine.' But Packie knows he isn't right. He went to see Mick Byrne who told him he would have to go tell Jack that he couldn't play.

So Packie goes in to see Jack. By now we all know he's not playing. He walks into Jack's room. 'Well what can I do for you, Packie? What's the matter?' So Packie tells Jack that his back is not right – 'I can't do this, I can't do that and I don't want to let the lads down.' Jack stops him in his tracks. 'Well if you don't play you will let the lads down, you'll let me down. Anyway, I've just seen you out there and you could catch the ball. You're all right.' That was it. Packie had gone in to tell Jack he didn't feel right for the biggest game he has ever played in, and a couple of minutes later he walks out and tells the lads that he IS playing!

I was nervous on the morning of the match, Saturday, June 18. So nervous that I went to have a haircut. A lot of the others were up early, and Mick Byrne was busy – a sure sign that there are a few nerves about. Of course Kevin Moran and Paul McGrath were still in bed. They sacrificed breakfast for a few more hours between the sheets. We left for the stadium at about twelve noon. I couldn't believe the amount of orange we could see on the way to the stadium. All of Holland seemed to have made the trip to Gelsenkirchen for the match. We were playing a game of 'Spot the Irish supporter' there was so much orange. Then, when we got to the stadium and we were going in, I looked back down the main avenue leading up to the stadium and it was packed with orange. But there, right in the middle of it all was a single German policeman on a horse – and on the back of the horse was a lone Irish supporter proudly waving the tricolour. It was a wonderful moment, the Irish were coming.

I didn't want to go out for a warm-up because the nerves were getting to me. From coming to Germany as the 'pub' team we were now on the brink of a place in the semi-finals of Euro'88. I finally decided to go out. There was an elevator up to the pitch and when I went up the place was already half-full with Dutch fans. I remember saying to one of the lads, 'Have the FAI not told the fans that we're playing here today?' But then I saw the little pocket of fans in a corner of the field.

Jack calmed us down and told us what we had to do before the game. 'They will have to come at us,' he said. 'They need the two points, we just need one. Keep it tight, don't let them settle and we'll be here for another few days.' We played according to plan for the first forty-five minutes and we should have scored. Paul McGrath saw the best chance of the first half come back off their upright. Chris Hughton was playing brilliantly and Ruud Gullit didn't get a look in against him. Chris Morris in the other fullback berth got a dig in the eye, but he was playing out of his skin too. We went in at half-time with the score at 0-0.

They had caused us few problems. They were, however, getting to the line. They were getting in crosses but we were clearing them, we were defending fairly competently. Big Packie, despite his bad back, had made a couple of good saves. So Jack gets at us. 'You've got forty-five minutes left, you can hold them, there's no reason why they should score,' he said. 'But we're letting them have a little bit too much play and we're not inflicting our game on them.' Jack knows we are all knackered. We have played two tough games already in one week. Jack tries to put us at ease. Just keep it the same, just keep defending, stop them getting the ball through the middle. But overall he's happy with us – just a few little things that might be causing us problems.

We were cruising through the second half. We weren't causing them any problems, but we were defending well. Chris Hughton still had Gullit in his pocket. Chris Morris had had to come off at half time however, as his eye had almost closed by now and Paul McGrath moved back to right full. He had a wonderful game there, nobody was getting past him.

And by now the Dutch are pumping the high ball in towards Kevin Moran and myself. That's like bread and butter to us. We could have stood there all day and cleared the ball if they continued that. We were hanging on and then tragedy struck. One of the lads cleared our lines with a header and it fell to Ronald Koeman. He hit it back in, but it was always going wide – until Wim Kieft managed to get his head to it and diverted it past Packie. They had scored with just eight minutes remaining. But the lads were magnificent. They got up and at the Dutch, forced a few corners and throw-ins. Finally, the clock ran out on us.

I went up to Gullit and exchanged shirts with him, wished him all the best for the rest of the tournament. He's a lovely chap and I had a little chat with him. Then we said a fond farewell to our supporters. Back in the dressingroom Jack tried to lift us. It was hard this time. We were all so upset with the result. We had started as outsiders then come so far, to be knocked out by a freak goal. Then one of the lads noticed Gullit's shirt and he says: 'Poor bastard, Gullit is probably going around his dressingroom wanting to know who owns this Irish shirt?' By the time we got back to the hotel the gloom was beginning to lift. We helped each other to forget it. And that night we had the usual – a sing-song and a few beers. We were looking forward to going home to Dublin as heroes.

HOMECOMING

On the way to the airport our special tape goes on. I don't know how it started but we always play it now on the way to a game. We always had music on the bus, but some of it was very slow, mournful stuff. So Jack got on the bus one day and said: "Get that bloody thing off, it's like going to a funeral, it's like a wake." So the tape was changed to 'Molly Malone', 'The Boys In Green' and 'Sean South from Garryowen'. Now everybody, including Jack, sings the songs on the way to the stadium. Singing along to the tape breaks the monotony and helps us get geed-up for a match. The first time I used that tape it proved to be a lucky omen, we had a good result – so we've kept it up since then.

Charlie O'Leary was in charge of the tape one time. 'Sean South' *has* to be playing as we enter the stadium. And if Charlie doesn't get the sequence right then he's in real trouble: 'Get the f…king tape on Charlie. You little bastard it's the wrong one' are just some of the remarks thrown at the little man. And Charlie is up-front and the wrong tape will come on – once it was 'Humpty Dumpty' and all the lads roared at him. Then if 'Sean South' comes on too early the bus driver gets some stick and is told to slow the bus down or hurry up!

When we arrived at the airport most of the lads are still bevied from the night before and still hyper from our night out. Then the madness begins. The film 'Blind Date' was doing the rounds at the time and in one scene Kim Bassinger is in a restaurant and she just rips the pocket off somebody's jacket. We were all wearing our green Euro'88 blazers and one of the lads just walked up to another and R-I-P! his breast pocket was gone. Another breast pocket goes, then another. By now everybody is hanging on to their breastpockets – if they still have one. So the sidepockets start going! And now you've got a problem, you can't hold all three. Then it gets ridiculous. Somebody ripped the arm off a jacket. The fun continues on the plane. The hostesses are pouring out champagne for the lads and Tony Galvin is going around telling everybody to leave his blazer alone. Tony had promised to give it to his grandfather. We respected that – but nobody else was safe – especially John Aldridge. We decided that it was all Aldo's fault, so he had the collar, sleeves and finally anything that was left ripped off his shirt.

We arrived back in Dublin to unbelievable scenes. We had been told there were a lot of people to welcome us home, but we were thinking: Well, they'll greet us at the airport and then we'll be off. But the airport was mobbed. We hadn't expected anything like this at all. We were mobbed all the way down to O'Connell Street, around Parnell Square and up to the Municipal Gallery for a civic reception. We managed to get everybody to be quiet for a few minutes and sang 'Molly Malone' for them. It was our tribute to the fans who had travelled to the Championships. They had gone out there tarred with the same brush as the English supporters. The locals in Stuttgart, Hanover and Gelsenkirchen were sceptical of our fans at first but the fans soon won them over. They went to Germany to enjoy themselves and support their team. We were already close to our fans, but the European Championships tied the knot even tighter.

The European Championships also put me in the shop window and played a prominent part in my transfer from Glasgow Celtic to Olympique Lyon in France.

THE WORLD CUP

WORLD CUP QUALIFIERS

IN MANY OTHER EUROPEAN COUNTRIES the European Championships of 1988 were just a memory by the time the qualifying tournament for Italia'90 kicked off in September 1988. Everywhere, that is, except the Republic of Ireland. Our exploits in Germany just three months earlier had lifted the country, and now we were expected to qualify for the big one, the World Cup, by our army of fans. We had been drawn in European Group Six with Spain, Hungary, Malta – and Northern Ireland. Two teams would go through to the finals in Italy in 1990. Jack and all the lads felt we could make it and write another chapter in Irish soccer history by becoming the first team to do so.

Jack pulled a masterstroke, although his critics might have described it as more of a master gamble. We would play Northern Ireland, Spain and Hungary away, before playing a World Cup game in Dublin at Lansdowne Road. If we could collect some points from those fixtures then we would have four matches at home before travelling to Malta for our last qualifying group match.

NORTHERN IRELAND

Before we even kicked a ball against Northern Ireland in Belfast there were problems. The Irish Football Association (IFA) in their wisdom decided that it would be better if no supporters travelled from the south for the match. So when we travelled north by plane the day before the match – Tuesday, September 13, 1988 – we knew that we wouldn't have their magnificent support at Windsor Park the following night.

HIGH SECURITY

When we arrived at the airport there was strict security. A few detectives got on board our bus and with an armed escort we were driven to a beautiful hotel on the outskirts of the city. Later that evening we travelled to Windsor Park for a training session. This time the security was even tighter. Even while we trained that evening a helicopter hovered over Windsor Park. The lads of course cracked on about it. One wag in the squad decided that Northern Ireland boss Billy Bingham was in the 'copter on a spying mission.

We did the usual training that evening – a few exercises and a little knockabout game to loosen us up a bit and get rid of any cobwebs.

I can remember feeling a little tense before the match because we expected to beat them or get a result anyway after the European Championships. The next evening we set off for Windsor Park at around 6pm, and again it was the full security bit. Then Charlie O'Leary stepped forward and slipped on our favourite pre-match bus journey songs. Then it dawned on him – 'Sean South From Garryowen' might not go down too well in this part of the world!

But the security blokes were fine. They said, 'No, no, work away, play what you like', but they did ask us to turn it down a little as we sped through one particularly Loyalist area. Despite all that we were still fairly relaxed and in the dressingroom Jack just did his little bit, talked to a few players and told us that we were more than capable of getting a result on the night.

The atmosphere was hostile to say the least. There were a lot of remarks, none of them complimentary. Then there was Jack. He was walking up along the track and he was getting all the verbals: 'You long-necked f…ker and English traitor' – all the usual, moronic comments that bigots make. And Jack walked to the fence, stuck his head through it and cadged a cigarette off one of them! It was amazing but it diffused the situation and, anyway, that kind of thing just rolls off Jack like water off a duck.

We enjoyed most of the play that night and should have come away with more than a point. Big Packie wasn't there, he had just had a back operation after the European Championships and Gerry Peyton deputised in goal. Gerry doesn't get many games because of Packie but whenever he's called upon he never lets himself or anybody else down. That night was no different. He hadn't much to do but when he was needed he was there and made three or four important saves.

Tony Cascarino had one effort that seemed to cross the line but the French referee ruled it out and Ray Houghton, after a great run, had the ball hooked off the line. We took a point as the game ended 0-0 – but on reflection we should have won.

SPAIN (SEVILLE)

Two months later, almost to the day, we were in Seville in southern Spain for what looked, on paper, like our hardest away match in the group. We flew out from Manchester on Monday, November 14, and then had over an hour's drive to our hotel – and it took us over an hour to get from there to the stadium for training and back on Tuesday afternoon.

We had got off to a bad start because we were short, through injuries, of Chris Hughton, Paul McGrath, Ronnie Whelan, Kevin Sheedy, Frank Stapleton and Liam Brady. It was also the only time, in four years, that I disagreed with Jack's team selection. He had always said that the strongest part of his team was his defence and he broke it up that night when he moved Kevin Moran into midfield, replacing him with David O'Leary. I could understand that Jack was struggling because of the list of injuries but I had a special relationship with Kev in defence.

Steve Staunton came in that night for what was only his second cap. It was a big match to come into. Spain had never been beaten in front of their fanatical supporters at the Benito Villamarin Stadium in Seville. They had lost the odd match in Madrid, but never in Seville. They are a volatile crowd there, almost intimidating because of their fanaticism.

We defended well for the first half-hour. But we were not comfortable with so many changes. We became a little disjointed and paid for it. The Spaniards sensed we weren't too happy and went for the jugular. They got two goals and we were lucky to escape with just a 2-0 defeat. It could have been 4-0 or 5-0. Now Jack's critics were questioning his plan to play so many away fixtures at first in our group. We were down three points out of a possible four and the vultures were closing in. But their criticisms only made us more determined to qualify for the finals in Italy.

HUNGARY (AWAY)

We had four months to mull over what went wrong in Spain before we met Hungary in Budapest in March 1989. We had dropped three points, so what? There was still a long way to go in the group, another six games to be exact, and after the Budapest match we had four of them at home. Jack kept making that point as we flew out on Monday, March 6: Get something out of this game and we're back on the trail. What our critics tended to forget was that less than two years before, a draw in Belfast and a 2-0 defeat in Seville would have meant success! But, for them, 'success should breed success'. They were still on our backs, and it was to get worse after the match against Hungary.

Going into the match against Hungary that March night some important things had to be remembered: just two short years before an Irish team getting *any* result away from home was rarer than finding a leprechaun at the end of a rainbow, winning the lottery, or finding Mick McCarthy doubling up with Lord Lucan on the back of Shergar outside Mount Mellick! Jack had an advantage over Johnny (Giles) and Eoin (Hand) … he was a foreigner with no idea of what went before.

So we went out that Wednesday night, March 8, 1989 and played Hungary off the pitch. We should have beaten them but we didn't score and it ended up 0-0. They didn't have a real chance all night, and we were bitterly disappointed after the game that we didn't win. Two or three years earlier such a result would have been met with banner headlines back home. This time we were hammered for only drawing! But the fans, the real fans who travelled all the way across Europe, knew that we were back on course for a place in the World Cup finals.

SPAIN (HOME)

Now we were back in Dublin, a place that no other team in the world liked to visit by now. In between our World Cup matches we had played Tunisia in October 1988 (4-0) and France in February 1989 (0-0). They were happy to escape with those results. We had lost just one game in Dublin since Jack arrived, going down to Wales 1-0 in Jack's debut as manager in March 1986, and the only team that had given us the run around had been Spain in Seville in November 1988. Now they were coming to Dublin. As I said earlier we were short several key players when we played them in Seville. Now we had a full squad, and they had to play in front of our fans.

The players arrived in Dublin on the weekend of April 23. Partying on the Sunday was out the window for us. We had a point to prove against Spain, who were potentially the best team in our group. All of the players were infected by the buzz around Dublin that weekend and on the day leading up to match. It was very much a case of 'Your country expects', but without all those heavy overtones. When the lads went into town on Monday to do some shopping the atmosphere was electric. Fans, aged six to sixty-six, came up to us, shook hands and wished us the very best. How could we let them down?

But we knew what it meant. If we were to lose to Spain, our World Cup dreams might be over. We also owed Spain one. Nobody could beat us and get away with it. I don't think anybody to this day knows how wound up we were for that game. Pride came into it in a BIG way. Even before the match in the dressingroom Jack didn't have to say too much. He could see that we just wanted to get out there and do a demolition job on the opposition. We were, to say the least, well wired up.

Jack also handed me the captaincy. I had captained the team before but now it was big time. There was no way I was going to relinquish it. I was proud to play for Ireland and now I had been given the extra honour of being captain. I intended to live up to the extra responsibility. I've got other very strong memories of that day. For a start I was hyper. I don't like being beaten, I don't like losing the toss before a match. As a matter of fact I'm a very bad loser, at anything. There's a picture of me shaking hands with Emilio Butragueno taken just before that match that tells the story. I'm squeezing his mitt and staring right through him: Emilio, this isn't a football match this is war; if we can get one over on you and your teammates then we're heading for Italy. Yes, I was that hyper – and our fans could sense it too.

Needless to say, it was a physical game from the start. Within minutes Sanchez Manolo is breaking through and I make a right crunching tackle on him and get booked. It was the best thing that could happen to me. Another warning and I was off, so it focused my mind on the job that had to be done. They were coming at me ten a minute, hoping that I would blow my top and end up getting sent off. But I was having none of that. This game was too important for the team and the fans. And then Butragueno started again. I put a tackle in and he was furious. He came up to me and started at me in his broken English: 'McCartee …' I just grabbed him with one hand around his chin and walked him away. He was disgusted, upset because we were playing our game, and getting on top.

Later when I watched the game on television, I could understand how he felt. We were like a pack of wolves. Balls were being pumped into their box, Big Cas was knocking them all over the place, and our lads could smell victory. It was only a matter of time before the pressure paid off and then we were one-up. It might have been an own-goal but it didn't make any difference to us. We were in front and that's all that mattered. They were totally rattled and it turned out to be one of those great days at Lansdowne. We were well and truly back in the race to Italy and everybody loved us that evening.

MALTA (HOME)

In May we were at home to Malta, a game I missed through injury. I was with Celtic at this time and on the previous Saturday we had beaten Rangers in the Scottish Cup final. After the match I went out for a few drinks with the players and we celebrated late into the night. On the Sunday, a week before the game against Malta, I went for a run just to keep the body ticking over. I hadn't trained too much prior to the Cup final because of the knee, but I felt guilty that morning because of the amount of alcohol that had been consumed during the celebrations after the final. I ran up the street and started to limp. I thought, this is sore. I had got about 150 yards and I should have worked any pain out, but instead it got worse. I turned back and walked to my house. By the time I got to the house I was limping heavily and decided to have an op on the knee.

By now, of course, World Cup fever had hit Ireland with a vengeance. The match against Malta was on Sunday, May 28, and Packie told me later that the buzz in Dublin that weekend was amazing. And the buzz obviously affected the Maltese because goals from Ray Houghton and Kevin Moran secured two points for us.

HUNGARY (HOME)

The following Sunday, Hungary were the visitors to Lansdowne Road. I flew over for that match because I wanted to be part of things with the lads. Packie was right. The atmosphere in Dublin was something else.

Ireland played really well and never looked like losing. Paul McGrath scored early on to take some of the pressure off us and then Packie made a tremendous save shortly after we scored. If the Hungarians had pulled back a goal at that stage it would have put the pressure back on, but Packie, as usual, pulled a save out of the top drawer to get us out of trouble. Then, late in the second half, Tony Cascarino was rewarded for all his hard work in the previous games when he put the game beyond the Hungarians with a headed goal. Now the picture was somewhat different – five points out of eight ... Here we go, here we go.

FRIENDLY AGAINST GERMANY

Jack had begun his World Cup preparations before we qualified, with a friendly match in September 1989 against West Germany. Although missing some of their Italian-based players, the Germans were still formidable opposition. We began the game with a real flourish and Frank Stapleton struck with a great opportunist's goal. We were all over them after that but we couldn't break them down again. Then they hit back, with a magnificent goal, a shot from outside the area that gave Packie no chance at all.

At half-time Jack gave us a real roasting. He was annoyed we let them back into the game having competed so well up to then. The equaliser had come around the time when Jack pulled off Liam Brady and replaced him with Andy Townsend. The boss felt we were getting the runaround down Liam's side and their winger was causing Steve Staunton all kinds of problems because he wasn't getting enough cover. Bringing on Andy was Jack's plan to strengthen up that side of the field.

In the second-half we put them under pressure again but they were well organised. I was very impressed with them – their slow build-up, sometimes a build-up that was almost boring. But then as the game moved into its final quarter they began to play it across the back to keep possession. The final score, 1-1, was a good result for us. If I was a betting man I would have stuck a few punts on them to win the World Cup I was that impressed with them. I'm a bit sorry now that I didn't!

They showed us a lot of respect by coming to play us in Dublin. They came because we were, their manager Franz Beckenbauer felt, the best team at playing that type of game. Beckenbauer was full of praise for us after the game and said he hoped we wouldn't be drawn in the same group in Italy. And Franz made my day in the tunnel before the game when he said, 'Hello Mick, how are things?' and stuck out his hand to shake. I was really made up. He is a real hero of mine, one of the truly great footballers and a great manager – and besides all that my wife Fiona fancies him as well!

Between March and May 1990 we played three other friendlies leading up to the World Cup – against Wales, the USSR and Finland. These were the games where Jack assessed his squad, but I believe he knew from early on who would be going to Italy with him.

NORTHERN IRELAND (DUBLIN)

We had almost four months to wait for the return clash with Northern Ireland at Lansdowne. In between, their World Cup aspirations had all but disappeared with a series of bad results. We knew we could take them, but they weren't going to lie down and let us walk all over them. It would be a feather in their cap if they could put one over on us. We knew they were going to lift their game, play twice as hard. There was a lot of pride at stake. The press hyped the match up. They said that Northern Ireland still had a chance of qualifying for Italy. That was a load of crap. They would have to win the rest of their games handsomely. They had nothing to lose while we had everything to lose.

By the time Wednesday, October 11, came around the tension everywhere was high. A friend of mine who was going to work that morning said that you cut it with a knife in O'Connell Street. The tension was combined with a little apprehension. This was something like a derby game, and we all know what *they* can be like – dour, unattractive and with the underdogs playing out of their skins. Winning against Northern Ireland meant so much to everybody connected with the team – the fans, the players, the whole country. We were on the brink of a place in the World Cup finals and it could all slip away from us if they won. But the tension ended for the players as soon as the game started.

However, you could see we were nervous as soon as the first ball was kicked. It affects you in many ways. Your legs seem to be heavy, your passing is not as crisp as it should be and you feel unfit when you are actually a 100 per cent. The Northern Ireland team could sense it.

They got into the game much quicker and caused a few problems early on. Norman Whiteside was booked after about five minutes. He was so hyped up for the match, he wanted to win it so desperately. He's a great competitor and had just returned to international football and wanted to prove a point. But he was putting the tackles in everywhere and the referee had to step in. But even the booking didn't take the edge off his game. They had the best of the first-half encounters. We were struggling.

Indeed, they should have taken the lead. Colin Clarke was up-front trying to get a flick on a ball to release one of their players. He managed it once and Michael O'Neill, a very talented player, got onto the end of it. Luckily he miscontrolled it, which allowed me time to tap his arm – an old pro's trick – which put him off for a split second and that allowed Packie to come out and clear his lines.

But the ball was played back in again, and this time we were really in trouble. I don't know who it was who got to the ball but he should be shot for missing it. He had an open goal and scoring then would have really put the cat among the pigeons. All he had to do was hit the thing and we would have been behind. I managed to get back and clear his feeble effort off the line. I remember thinking that if it had been Norman Whiteside in that position he would have put the ball, and me, in the back of the net. Big Norm would have made sure by blasting the thing home. Northern Ireland were playing well at the back then too so if that one had counted I don't really know if we would have come back from it. Then just before half-time, Ronnie

Whelan struck. Their goalkeeper, George Dunlop, came off his line and flapped a little and Ronnie just picked his spot and wham! we were one up. We went in at half-time ahead, the goal coming at a critically pyschological time for us. We had been on the rack and now we were ahead.

HALF-TIME

Jack said as much at half-time. It had taken us too long to get into the game. They had settled quickly and were playing some decent football. But Jack felt that the double blow they had suffered – not scoring and then letting one in, against the run of play, might have killed them off. We had no intention of letting them back into the game now. We came out a different team after the interval. We were all over them and Tony Cascarino, with a header, and Ray Houghton, with a wonderful strike, put the game beyond them. We were playing football now, knocking the ball around and the only surprise was that we didn't score a few more. Poor old John Aldridge ran himself into the ground and had a few chances, but, as usual, when it comes to playing for the Republic they just wouldn't go in for him.

But we were there, the World Cup finals in Italy beckoned. Dublin went wild. I couldn't get too carried away with the celebrations. I was now playing for Olympique Lyon and the president of the club had flown over in his private jet for the match. Within two hours of the final whistle I was on my way back to France with him.

Technically Hungary could still go through. But for that to happen Malta, our last game in the group, would have to beat us something like 6-0 and Hungary would also have to beat Spain, in Seville. That was never going to happen. It might seem a little blasé to say that. But I knew we weren't going to let it slip away from us now.

MALTA (AWAY)

Once again injury was to rob me of a place for the game against Malta in November 1989. I was having trouble with the knee and I didn't think Lyon would release me to go out even to watch the game. I went to see Raymond Domenech and explained my situation. He was wonderful. 'Of course you must go,' he said. 'You are the captain and you have to be there when Ireland makes history.' He was great about it. They didn't have to let me go. But, as I've said before, Lyon were very good to me. He shooed me away from him to go and make my travel arrangements.

So I flew out to Malta on Tuesday, November 14, the day before the match. There was a carnival atmosphere on the island. The fans had come for a celebration party and on Tuesday they were already celebrating the celebrations that were to come the following day! I made my way down to the Rabat Stadium to watch our Under-18 team take on the Maltese. But the fella on the gate wouldn't let me in. I tried to explain to him that I was with the team, but he wasn't having any of that. The fans soon let him know. 'Jaysus, that's Mick McCarthy' was the cry and finally the gate-keeper bowed to public demand. The fans had something concrete to celebrate that evening because the Under-18 team won 1-0.

No matter how confident you are about beating a team there is always the nagging suspicion that the opposition might just nick a result. That's what Jack said to the players before the match. 'Go out and do a job. Be professional and treat them as any other team – with a little respect. If you think all you have to do is go out on the pitch you might end up getting a very painful kick in the nuts.' When the lads ran out to play that afternoon, I was sick I wasn't out there with them. I had missed the previous game against Malta and the tie against Hungary, but had been in for the two big home matches against Spain and Northern Ireland. But this was the real 'biggy', the day Ireland qualified officially. I wanted so much to be part of it. I was also brassed off because that was the day the 'official' World Cup poster picture was taken and I wasn't in it. They did superimpose my mug on the poster at the bottom, but it's not the same. You want to be standing up there with the lads.

The match was scrappy. Malta worked very hard. But the only way they were going to get anything out of it was if we were unprofessional in our approach, and that wasn't going to happen that day – good old Aldo made sure of that with a great far-post header in the first-half and a penalty after half-time when Andy Townsend was impeded going through. We won 2-0 and we were well and truly on our way to Italy. The jubilance of the fans in the stadium was hard to describe.

The feeling for the team, of the players for each other, for Ireland. Now it was time to have the biggest party that Malta has ever seen. We had qualified in style, conceding just those two goals to Spain in Seville. We had every reason to have a party.

Back at the hotel that evening they had laid on a little reception for us. It was a *little* reception, and at 10 o'clock we got tossed out of it. We had to celebrate, so we hit the streets of St Julians and there were probably more people there that night than there were in Dublin.

We strolled around the bars to see the fans and we signed everything – and I mean everything. It was almost an hour before I got a drink because every time I went to order one, another fan wanted something signed. It was manic. In the end somebody gave me a big red felt pen and I just sat there signing. I had had enough of it eventually so I left that particular pub and went around the corner to another one. I wanted a drink but it wasn't to be. That pub was worse, so I ended up going back to the one I had started off in.

I thought, well, I've signed every autograph in the place so maybe now I can have a drink. I had a pint or two in relative peace and then this fella comes up to me and asks me for an autograph. It was, 'Will you sign this for me?' and I said, 'Look it, mate, I've signed everything already.' With that he said, 'You haven't signed my backside!' I said, jokingly, 'Well drop your trousers and I will' – and he did! So I signed his backside and said, 'That's it, I've signed EVERYTHING now' and threw the pen out into the car park. Needless to say there were more autographs, but we had a little fun with that one. I don't know if he's still carrying my name around on his rear end to this day!

LIAM BRADY'S FINAL IRELAND GAME

Our final warm-up game was against Finland on May 16. It was to be Liam Brady's testimonial and the last time he would play for the Republic. It was also going to be a party, as the fans lined up to give us a rousing send-off on the road to Italy. But Finland never read the script properly and nearly ruined the party! We hadn't been beaten at Lansdowne for over four years. It was one of the best international records in the world. But at times it weighed heavily on us. We were going to get beaten some time and the longer the record stood the more pressure there was. Ironically, before the game Jack spoke about

*: PUSH AND SHOVE – light moment during [tra]ining in Cagliari. Big [Jack] is the first person to enjoy a joke.

[Ri]ght: RAY STOOPS TO [CONQ]UER – Ray Houghton [get]s a head to the ball in [the E]uropean Champion-[sh]ips against England, and we're ahead!

Above: WOULD YOU BUY A SECOND-HAND CAR FROM THIS MAN?
– A "youngish" Mick McCarthy joins the ranks of the Republic of Ireland soccer squad

Opposite top: JIG OF JOY – I don't think I've ever seen Ronnie Whelan jump so high … but who could blame him after scoring a stunner against the Soviet Union in Germany?

Left: OOH, AH, PAUL McGRATH – Paul's effort, our best against Holland in Euro '88, comes back off an upright

Above: OLÉ, OLÉ – My World Cup room-mate Frank Stapleton wheels
away after putting the Spanish goalkeeper "under pressure" during the
qualifying match in Dublin
Below: WHEN IRISHMEN CLASH – Getting the better of Colin Clarke in
the World Cup qualifier against Northern Ireland in Dublin

HIS MASTER'S VOICE – Big Jack discussing tactics in Italy in the most beautiful of settings at Terrasini in Sicily. Even at the training grounds the fans turned up to cheer us on!

Above: MY PROUDEST MOMENT – Leading out the Irish team against England in our first ever World Cup finals match left me with a lump in my throat. Here I'm showing the lads how it's done

Below: THE EAGLE HAS LANDED – Ray Houghton appears to be landing to ruffle the feathers of Egyptian Hani Ramzy

Above: MY BALL – My partner at the back doing what he's best at … Kevin Moran gets in first to clear the ball as Holland's Ruud Gullit advances in our vital Group F match in Palermo

Left: PUSH OFF – Big Cas gives Holland's Ronald Koeman the brush during our 1-1 World Cup draw

Opposite top: THE HANDS OF GOD – Big Packie takes off in the Stadio Luigi Ferraris

Left: CATCH OF THE DAY – Packie's save from Timoftei helps us into the World Cup quarter-finals

Above: DIDN'T HE DO WELL – Packie enjoys the moment as the stadium erupts ... and the whole of Ireland went wild as well

Above: WE'RE THERE – Andy Townsend turns to the fans
in joyous mood after the penalties

Below: CELEBRATIONS, IRISH STYLE – Underneath this mound of players
is David O'Leary after his penalty strike against Romania

Above: WITH GOD ON OUR SIDE – One of the real highlights of Italia '90 was our audience with the Pope – the only team to be granted one

Below: BEFORE THE FINAL BATTLE – Ronnie Whelan and Chris Morris enjoy a joke during training in Rome

Top: A MOMENT FULL OF PRIDE – Big Jack, Dave O'Leary, Charlie O'Leary and Mick Byrne stand for the national anthem in Rome's Olympic stadium

Above: OI! WHERE ARE YOU GOING? – Andy Townsend keeps tabs on Italian skipper Guiseppe Bergomi

Above: SICILIAN STRIKE – Toto Schillaci is there to slot the ball home and end our World Cup dreams

Right: THE LAST GOOD-BYE – The fans wouldn't leave the Olympic Stadium until Jack made a last appearance … a moment he says he will never forget

Left: HOME THE HEROES – We knew the fans were going to greet us when we got back to Dublin. But we never expected anything quite like this
Above: A REAL IRISH WELCOME – Only the Pope had more people turn out to see him. The team crawls past Dublin's O'Connell Monument
Below: THANK YOU ONE AND ALL – Jack and myself thank the fans in College Green, Dublin, followed by a few rousing bars of Molly Malone

Above: GENERALS OF GENOA – The team that started against Romania (back row): Niall Quinn, Andy Townsend, Packie Bonner, Paul McGrath, Mick McCarthy, Steve Staunton. (Front row): Kevin Moran, John Aldridge, Kevin Sheedy, Chris Morris, Ray Houghton

Below: AT HOME IN KENT – Fiona with Mick and Anna (7), Michael (3) and Katie (5)

it. Of course he wanted to win, he hates to lose. But he added that if we were going to be beaten in the near future then make it now, before the World Cup. Lose the record against Finland, but let's beat England, Egypt and Holland!

For all the lads the game came almost immediately after a long season. The Finns set about us and we just couldn't get going. We were off form, we weren't thinking about the game and the longer it went on the more the Finns came into the game. I knew I wasn't playing well. Mixu Paatelainen was having a great game against me. The Dundee United striker probably won everything in the air that day. After a half an hour or so we knew that we were in a game and began to pull ourselves together. Had we scored then we would have massacred them, but they managed to hold out to half-time.

The game became very scrappy over the final forty-five minutes. Then, out of the blue, they mounted an attack. The ball came across and I got a reasonably good header to it, but it fell to a Finn and he just flicked it up and volleyed it, straight as a bullet past Packie and into the net. We're down 1-0 at Lansdowne and time is running out! Our unbeaten record is going down the toilet. It was the kick up the backside that we needed. Finland were not going to take our record away from us.

We began to play, the fans roared us on and we bombarded Finland until Kevin Sheedy scored. We could have won it then, but that would not have been a fair result on the day because the Finns had come and given us a great workout. Jack wasn't too worried afterwards. He knew the mental condition of the players going into the game and made allowances for that.

The point that Jack did make was that the game lasts ninety minutes. If you don't play for ninety minutes then you leave yourself open to getting beaten.

For Liam Brady it was a very emotional day. He was introduced to the fans before the game and they gave him a tremendous ovation. And he played well before Jack finally substituted him. He played some beautiful passes – his delicate touch and brilliant footballing brain were still there. But now he was gone. He had kicked his last ball for the Republic. If ever there was a player for budding youngsters to look up to, then Liam Brady is the one.

I'd like to finish the way Liam did – there's not many who do, there are hundreds and thousands that fall by the wayside, or just make a living out of the game. But they don't have the profile that Liam's had. He deserves every penny he's got for his talent – but also for the way he conducts himself. A very nice man.

WE'RE ON OUR WAY TO ITALY

THE FIRST WORLD CUP MATCH AGAINST ENGLAND was almost a month away but Jack had decided to take us away to Turkey for a game and then on to Malta to prepare for the finals. We spent a few days in Dublin buying last-minute items and enjoying what was to be our last hours of freedom before getting down to the hard work of preparing for the finals.

The squad had been picked and the only surprise was the inclusion of my Millwall teammate Gary Waddock. It was a wonderful surprise. You won't meet a quieter or nicer person in an Irish squad. Gary is a real gentleman and I was very pleased for him. As a youngster he had some great years with Queens Park Rangers and seemed destined for a regular place in the Irish team until tragedy struck in 1985 when he was just twenty-three. A bad injury cut short his career. He was on the scrapheap. But Gary fought back magnificently. He pushed himself through the pain barrier and fought hard to get back into the game. His fighting spirit didn't go unnoticed and the Belgian club Charleroi helped him resurrect his career. He rewarded them by helping them back into the Belgian First Division. Then, after a couple of seasons there, Tony Cascarino brought him to the attention of Millwall and Gary was back in the Football League. Now, after a surprise recall from Jack against the Soviet Union in April, he was on his way to the World Cup finals – a fairytale story if there was ever one.

JACK LAYS DOWN THE LAW

The night before we left for Turkey the International Airport Hotel laid on a special dinner for us. It was really nice – champagne, the works. That was the night that Jack laid down the law, the ground rules for our Italian trip. He also gave us a bit of a volley about the FAI-players' pool negotiations which had made all the headlines in the newspapers. It was a bit unfortunate that the details of the row between the players' pool representatives and the FAI had been made public. But by then it had been resolved. Yet Jack didn't like what had happened. He wasn't having player power in his team or squad. He was mad over the whole thing.

The pressure was on now: and Jack tore into us with the rules: If we wanted to go anywhere we had to ask; there would be no big nights out until the World Cup was over for us; this was not a holiday we were going on and the next two weeks were for training, hard training, to get us into condition for what lay ahead in Sardinia and Sicily; and if we wanted to see our wives then he would decide when we could! Jack had never talked like this before. Things like this had never been mentioned before and then all of a sudden he is laying down the law about training kit, what tracksuits we will wear. The pressure was definitely on and Jack was feeling it too. But what he wanted to say more than anything was that this was the BIG ONE and let's not let ourselves down.

Before we left, Jack was also worried about a couple of niggling injuries so he called Ronnie Whelan, Kevin Moran and Ray Houghton into a room and asked them would they be okay for the tournament. They all said Yes, so then Jack called in Mick Byrne, the physio. He asked him what did he think and Mick said they would be okay. Jack told Mick he knew he would say that, because he mollycoddled the players! He was right. Mick treats the players as if they were his own children. He cares for them like his own family. But Jack respected his word and that was that.

TURKEY

On Friday, May 23, we got a wonderful early morning send-off from Dublin Airport and after a journey that seemed to last a lifetime we finally arrived in Izmir, Turkey. Jack had taken us there to prepare us for the heat we would have to contend with in Italy, and boy was he right. We played Turkey on Sunday and I don't think I have ever played in such heat in all my life. It was 100 degrees in the stadium that Sunday afternoon and just a ten- or twenty-yard run and your shirt was wringing. It was the worst game you've ever seen, a goalless draw played out in the worst conditions. But everybody came through it and there were no injuries, which was the most important thing. The following morning, at an ungodly hour, we set off for Malta which was to be our training camp for the next two weeks.

MALTA

THE JOURNEY FROM IZMIR WAS UNEVENTFUL – long, boring, but uneventful. At the airport in Malta the lads were amusing themselves going around on the luggage conveyor. I was sitting with Bernie Slaven and Niall Quinn when I saw Jack call Gary Waddock aside. I saw the look on Gary's face. I knew what Jack was saying to him but I hoped I was wrong. He was pulling Gary out of the squad. Jack stood talking to Gary for ages, and you could see Gary was disappointed to say the least. It was probably the hardest decision Jack has ever had to make. It was also a heartbreaking time for Gary. The fairytale that had started just a week before had now turned into a nightmare. But Jack wasn't doing it out of any malice. He felt that the way things stood at the time he needed more options, so he was going to replace Gary. Alan McLoughlin was the most likely replacement, but we weren't too sure yet. Gary was asked to stay on for the World Cup as a guest of Jack and the FAI, but Gary didn't know what to do. He needed time to think, so he travelled on to Malta with us to mull over it. The flight was subdued because of what had happened. We didn't know how to console Gary. What do you say to somebody in a situation like that?

The hotel in Malta was in the middle of nowhere. As soon as we arrived there we knew it wasn't going to be any holiday. There was nothing to do in the place. It seemed run-down and we complained a bit. It was then we found out that the place had been shut for years and had re-opened only recently. Jack thought it was great. 'It's a great place,' he said. 'I stayed here with Pat [his wife] about eight years ago. You'll love it.' My answer to him was simple. 'It might have been nice then, but I betcha it closed the week after you left.' So there was no drinking allowed and the lads began to play a game almost immediately – they re-named the place the 'Betty Ford Clinic'. The food wasn't the best when we arrived either, and the portions were small, very small. FAI official Eddie Corcoran, who had been a chef, was dispatched to the kitchen to sort things out. Eddie ended up with the job for the rest of the trip – he was chief liaison officer between the grub and the team's intestines.

Training started almost immediately. Jack ran us into the ground in the morning, then it was off to the stadium in the afternoon for some football, then back to the 'Clinic' for maybe an hour's sunbathing and then it was time for dinner. Dinner was now one of the highlights of the day – it broke up the monotony of things. Ironically, Jack had picked Malta so that we could acclimatise. But for the first few days it did nothing but pour rain while they were having a heatwave back in Dublin!

By now Gary had decided to go home. He couldn't bear being there but not part of things. He came around and wished us all the very best. He took it with such dignity, just like the man he is. It was so sad really, but Jack had to do what he felt was right for the team. Alan McLoughlin was his replacement sure enough, and his story was the other side of the coin from Gary's. On Monday, May 27, he had scored the only goal for Swindon against Sunderland in their play-off for a place in the First Division at Wembley. Alan literally shot Swindon into Division One for the first time in their career and now he was to play in the World Cup. There can't have been a happier man in British football. In the space of just six days I had seen it all – the depths of despair in Gary's case and sheer elation in Alan's case.

The game, on Saturday, June 3, was to have been a friendly behind closed doors against Malta. But the local association decided to throw the gates open to the public and had a crowd of about 3,000 at the game. The game meant nothing but was notable for one thing – Frank Stapleton, my roommate on tour, scored his twentieth goal for his country to set a new scoring record. It was also Alan McLoughlin's debut and we won handsomely 3-0, with the other goals coming from Niall Quinn and Andy Townsend.

Now it was back to training, training – and more training. And after training there was nothing to do back at the hotel, so card schools were set up and again John Aldridge was losing his shirt! Then, one night while flitting through the stations on the television one of the lads found an Italian programme called 'Tutti Frutti'. You didn't need to know too much of the lingo to understand the show. It was some kind of game show – and every night the hosts would end up stripping! So, after the word went around, the lads would slope off to their rooms around 9pm every night. It was 'Oh, that's it, I think I'll have an early night' and other such shoddy excuses.

Our journey each day to the training ground in the afternoon meant a ride on local coaches. They were sparse but very clean. I got on one afternoon and I remember I had just had some treatment, so I went to the back of the bus and got my feet up on another seat to rest the knee. The busman copped me in his mirror and walked down the bus. 'Why you have no respect for me' he screamed at me. I didn't know what was wrong with him, so I said something like 'What the f...k is the matter?' He flew into a huge rage. 'Why you have no respect for my bus and now you tell me to f...k?' I just took my foot down. Then he spotted one of the lads throwing a chewing gum paper on the floor. That was the biscuit for him. 'Why you have no respect for me and my bus?' he stormed. This bloke was paranoid. We had got on well with the Maltese, but you always get at least one odd-ball in the pack. And when someone opened one of the windows I thought he was going to blow a fuse. It was the same again, 'Why this' and 'Why that'. By this time all of us were fed up with him so it was a big 'F... OFF' from everyone. Needless to say, he didn't turn up the following day, but a chap who was obviously the boss arrived at the hotel to see Jack. He walked in to complain but ended up getting a earful from Jack, and that was that. We had a new bus driver the following day.

Near the end of our stay in Malta, Jack agreed to let us out for the night – a reward for good behaviour! We went down to a local bar and after about three pints I felt the worse for wear. I hadn't had a drop for over two weeks and it went straight to my head. I found a taxi and was back in my bed within a couple of hours. On June 8 we packed our bags and said *adieu* to the 'Betty Ford Clinic', and headed off to Sardinia and Cagliari. Our wonderful World Cup experience was about to begin.

SARDINIA

WE HAD BEEN AWAY FOR JUST OVER TWO WEEKS in Turkey and Malta preparing for the World Cup and now we were finally on the way to Italy. At Jack's meeting at the Dublin International Airport Hotel just before we left, the rules had been laid down about what we would have to do in Turkey and particularly Malta. I wouldn't say we were too happy about it – we all thought: Hold on Jack, we're not kids; we know what we have to do and we won't abuse things. But Jack was thinking ahead of us, just like a good chess player when you have to think three, four or five moves ahead of your opponent. Once again, Jack was right. We had trained hard and were in great condition as we boarded the plane for Sardinia.

The domestic season had finished almost a month previously. We should have been resting now, away on holidays with our families. But this was 1990, World Cup year, and nobody was complaining – because WE were there. The European Championships had put us on the map as a soccer nation for the first time in sixty-seven years since the FAI had become members of soccer's international governing body, FIFA. Now we were expected to DO things. Everybody back home thought we could get through our group and make the last sixteen in the World Cup finals. That would mean that the Republic of Ireland would be ranked, for the next couple of years anyway, as one of the top twenty soccer nations in the world – not bad for a country with just over 3.5 million inhabitants.

But we had to be prepared. We had to get fit again and ready after a long football season. It was the same for many of the other nations who had qualified. But some, like Egypt in our group, had selected players almost as soon as they qualified. They were then taken off as a squad and trained together for months. It was a bit different for the European teams. The season had just finished for us and it was up to the manager to lift his squad of players whichever way he thought best.

For Jack that meant getting away to Malta and working hard. It was almost like pre-season training all over again – and it worked. We arrived in Cagliari on Saturday, June 9, just raring to go. And it was then that we became part of the great World Cup show. As soon as we stepped off the plane it was television cameras and massive security. And the fans were there to welcome us too. We were ushered on to a coach – and after the bus in Malta this was paradise, heaven, nirvana! The seats were upholstered in blue leather, it was air conditioned, roomy and the driver was friendly. This was the big time. Security was something else, even tighter than when we made the trip to Belfast for our qualifying match. We had arrived. All the talk was about our clash with England and all we wanted to do was get on with it.

Our hotel was in a beautiful setting outside Cagliari. Actually it wasn't so much a hotel as a reception area with chalets set in a little wooded area which sloped down to the Mediterranean. But we had problems. The rooms were small, and so were the portions of food! Once again Eddie Corcoran was sent to the kitchens to get things right and he duly obliged. But even Eddie couldn't add another five or six square metres to the chalets.

Training was now toned down to a minimum. We were fit and our trips to the training grounds were simply to keep our bodies ticking over and for Jack to make sure nobody was carrying an injury. By now the media hype was also in full swing – after all it was Ireland versus England, the old enemy. England had a point to prove. Their fans wanted revenge for the European Championships. They felt there was no way Ireland could put one over on them again. One English newspaper interviewed our 'keeper Gerry Peyton and asked him how he felt about the English goalkeeper Peter Shilton. The following day it came out all wrong, with Gerry supposedly saying that Shilton was over the top and that the Irish team were not worried about him.

Gerry was incensed. You have to know the fella. He's a gentle giant and he wouldn't hurt anybody, and he certainly wouldn't have said what was printed in the paper that morning about a fellow professional. Goalkeepers are a breed unto themselves. They're close and they don't go around slagging each other. So Gerry rushed off a telegram to Peter and he, in turn, sent one back to Gerry. Shilton just said that he knew Gerry hadn't said anything like that and wished him all the best for the finals.

SELECTING THE TEAM

We did some light training on Saturday evening and then we all had an early night. On Sunday morning I took my usual swim. In Turkey I had got up early one morning for a dip and had continued to have one every morning after that while we were away. I had just finished when Jack approached me and I walked with him down to the rocks by the sea. He wanted to talk through the team with me, get my thoughts on it. He particularly wanted to discuss central defence and I thought: here we go, I'm out of the game against England. I had been injured after all and a lot of my critics were confident that I would be dropped. But Kevin had had an achilles tendon problem as well and Jack was just worried about who he should play at the back. Then Jack turned to me and asked me for my thoughts about the team. So I told him out straight.

Dave was certainly quicker than either Kevin or myself. He was also a classier footballer and he probably had more ability than either of us. That's what I told Jack. As regards stopping the ball, as defenders we were all on the same level. But Kevin and I had built up a partnership, a good partnership that had seen us through the European Championships. We had played together for so many matches that we had formed a strong bond, we had built up a great relationship on the pitch. When we played together we felt comfortable. It was a good partnership. Of course the final decision was up to Jack. He was the boss. As I joined the others for open-air mass that morning, Jack went off to try and finalise his team. The final selection for the match against England was lying heavy on his mind. Jack has this old hard-man image. But he's got a soft centre. He worries a lot about the squad. He wants everything to be right.

PRE-MATCH WAITING

We had our first sight of the Sant'Elia stadium in Cagliari that Sunday evening. We were relaxed and just had a little kickabout to get the feel of the place. We played a five-a-side match and then went back to the hotel to watch some of the games in the other groups. Already there had been shocks. In the first match of the tournament, Cameroon had beaten the defending champions Argentina 1-0, with just nine men. The previous evening, June 9, Italy had looked good when they defeated Austria by the same score, while Colombia had overcome the United Arab Emirates 2-0. That evening we watched Brazil defeat Sweden 2-1 and Czechoslovakia trounce the USA 5-1.

Now we were less than twenty-four hours away from playing against England and the nerves were beginning to act up a little. I could hear Mick Byrne moving between chalets asking players if they needed a sleeping tablet – there were several who accepted the offer.

But I had no time to think about the match that night. I was too busy trying to track my wife down on the island by telephone! We had left Malta on June 8 and Fiona was due to leave England for Sardinia the same day. She hadn't contacted me so I ended up telephoning her mother to find out if she had been in touch. Poor Fiona, everything had gone wrong for her. For a start nobody realised that there were two airports on Sardinia, one outside Cagliari, the other about 300 kilometres away. Then she had to drive down to Cagliari on not the best of roads, and finally the hotel she was staying in left a lot to be desired.

IRELAND/ENGLAND MATCH

Now it's the morning of the match. The tension is starting to build. Our clash is the first in Group F and the island is alive with anticipation. The day seems to slip by very slowly. The players try to keep their minds off the game by joking and playing cards. It seems to take ages before lunchtime comes around and then it's off for a snooze before we leave for the stadium. At 5pm there's a little light snack. We're all somewhat subdued. We have waited so long for this and now our first match in the World Cup finals is just hours away.

I suppose the enormity of it all had begun to dawn on us. Jack announced his team: Bonner, Morris, McCarthy, Moran, Staunton, McGrath, Townsend, Sheedy, Houghton, Cascarino and Aldridge. Kevin Moran was to play alongside me in defence. Jack had remained loyal to us once again.

It's all a bit of a blur after that – leaving our chalets, getting on the coach, moving off towards the stadium around 5.30pm. And then it hits us: the fans – English and Irish – the colour, and the atmosphere. Into the stadium, get changed and out on to the pitch for a little warm-up. It's just 7pm and already most of the Irish fans are in the stadium and they give us a great reception. The players are just beginning to realise fully the sense of history that's about to be created.

THE FANS

The English team had been out on the pitch a little earlier and had received a standing ovation – from the Irish fans! Their manager, Bobby Robson, was gobsmacked by it all. In over twenty-five years in the game he had never seen anything like it. Immediately after the match he sent a message to our officials asking them to pass his appreciation on to our supporters.

Now the time for battle is drawing near. Jack walks around the lads as we make our final preparations for the match. 'This is it,' he says. 'We fought hard for two years to get to this position.' It is tense, so then Jack does his usual: 'I'm glad they're playing Butcher and Robson (Bryan) – and Stevens at the back. And Waddle on the wing. Suits us fine,' he says. 'Great, they haven't learnt a lesson.' We smile and know what he's saying. Jack never does the 'Watch him he's great and be careful of him, he's very tricky' type of talk. He runs the other side down – if he can remember their names! Then he walks around to individual players and reminds them of what they have to do.

At 7.45pm we were out in the corridor lined up alongside the English team. Most of us know each other, we either play in the same teams or against one another week-in week-out in the Football League.

As we came out on the pitch the sound was deafening. England had plenty of support, but so had we. There were at least 10,000 Irish fans in the stadium and they made such a racket. We lined up for the national anthem – and then it hit me. As the fans sang the anthem I began to come to grips with what was happening. On a personal level, I had reached the stage which is every player's ambition by playing in the World Cup finals. As a youngster of fourteen or fifteen, when I had set my sights on becoming a professional footballer, I had dreamt about this. But now I was playing for the Republic against England, the country where I was born. There were absolutely no regrets. I was too proud wearing the green jersey for that. But I was also captain. I had led the Republic of Ireland out on to the pitch to play the old enemy England in their first ever World Cup finals match. I was so proud. I was proud for my father, my wife and my children. I was proud and delighted for the fans, for Jack, the rest of the team, and the rest of Ireland. And I thought of my mother. She had died five years previously of cancer. She would have been really proud of me now even though I was in an Irish shirt. There was a lump in my throat and I could even feel a few tears. I was so happy.

ENGLAND SCORES!

Now it was down to business. I won the toss – the one and only time during the finals – and elected to play the way we were. For the first few minutes both sides toyed with each other as we found our way. Then, before we could settle, England scored. Kevin Sheedy thought the ball had gone over the line and out of play to my left and raised his hand to let the referee know. But Chris Waddle wasn't waiting around to see what the referee was going to do. He swung over a great cross which flew over Kevin Moran's and my head. Gary Lineker was on it immediately. The ball bobbled in front of him and he seemed to stumble a little as Packie came out to collect it. But the bobble only helped Lineker, and caught Packie off balance. I had recovered and was closing in, but Lineker did just enough to slot it home. Just ten minutes were gone and we were behind. The debate still goes on in some circles as to whose fault the goal was. It wasn't Packie's. He did his best. We were, to a certain extent, caught off when Kevin Sheedy threw his arm in the air to signal the ball was out, but the cross was perfect. It caught me out and Chris Morris hadn't covered enough ground back into the penalty area to cover the space behind Kevin Moran and me. But in the final analysis Lineker was my man – it was my fault.

There was no time for recriminations. We had to haul ourselves off the floor straight away and get back into the game. And we did. After half an hour we were running things in midfield. Kevin Sheedy was superb and Paul McGrath, our best player in Italy, was inspired. They shut down English skipper Bryan Robson and Paul Gascoigne and we were beginning to make chances up-front.

At half-time we were expecting a right going over from Jack. But he just stood there and said we were playing well. We had hauled ourselves back into the game and if we continued to play the way we had since going behind, then everything would work itself out. We mustn't panic, he added. Just keep putting them under pressure and we would score.

THE EQUALISER

From the kick-off again we did just that. The ball was pumped into their third of the field all the time and the constant barrage began to make them uneasy. Then Sheedy struck. Steve McMahon was slow in clearing his lines and Kevin moved in and dispossessed him before firing an unstoppable shot across the face of Peter Shilton's goal. It was 1-1. Now we were chasing a winner. The lads were so hyped up, determined to show the world that our victory over England in the European Championships was no flash in the pan. The fans were manic. It was a non-stop chorus egging us on for the kill. Finally we ran out of time – but we had got a result and a point in our first match.

Sheedy walked off the park smiling like a Cheshire cat. He had come in for some stick over the years because some people thought he didn't work hard enough. But nobody could criticise his work rate that night. He was like a man possessed and deserved to be the one to put the ball past Shilton with that sweet left foot of his. Jack was obviously delighted too. 'We needed something out of that game, lads, and you got it,' he said as we came into the dressingroom. The pressure had lifted off his shoulders. He had been nervous right up to the kick-off but he wasn't going to let it show just in case it affected any of us.

Later I was told that several of the English players felt that they were unlucky not to win and that we hadn't caused them too many problems. Shilton went wild. 'I've played in over a hundred international matches and I have never been so busy or pressured in my life,' he screamed at them. I was also looking forward to the British newspapers the following morning to see what excuses they would come up with. After we played England in the European Championships one of the first excuses to come out was that Gary Lineker had hepatitis. Now Gary did have hepatitis, but he was only one player in a team of eleven. They just wouldn't give us any credit. What I wanted to find out this time was which one of them was injured or sick. Would it be Chris Waddle with gout or was Terry Butcher playing with one leg?

There wasn't going to be any party that night. 'A couple of beers back at the hotel and then bed. We have an early start in the morning,' said Jack. It always seemed to be an early start, and early usually meant any time before 7am. We had our dinner that evening and a few beers with it. But the lads wanted to celebrate because we had got off to such a great start and the pressure had lifted a little. So after dinner it was down to the hotel bar for a few more drinks. We were all as high as kites with our success. The word came down from Jack that we could stay up until 1am. He walked into the bar at 2.30am to get us all off to bed. He was annoyed. Not because we were late but because several of the players had brought their wives into the hotel. 'I told you about that,' he said. 'You will see your wives when I tell you, now get them out of the hotel and get to bed.'

Despite that, we were still on a high from the match. We had got a result against England. And I was so happy and proud. I had been captain of the Republic that night and that's a wonderful memory that will stay with me for the rest of my life.

PALERMO

UP THE FOLLOWING MORNING at the crack of dawn and after breakfast we were on the bus and off to the airport for the trip to Palermo in Sicily. We would be there in a matter of hours. For many of our supporters the journey would be a little longer, six to eight hours longer by bus and ferry. There was great media attention as soon as we hit the airport at Palermo. Another Italia'90 designer bus was there to meet us and whisk us away to our hotel on the outskirts of the town.

Once again we were in for a shock. The rooms were small (as usual), the food left a lot to be desired and, again, the portions were small. Eddie Corcoran was sent off to do his duty once more. But possibly the worst aspect was the air-cooling fans in the room. There was no air conditioning, just these huge fans that resembled the rotor blades of a helicopter and made almost as much noise. You couldn't sleep with the noise and if you turned them off you were drenched in sweat within minutes because of the heat and humidity. Most of the lads were a little under the weather after the night before. Training was optional that evening. As soon as dinner was out of the way we all gathered in the lounge to watch the match in Palermo's Stadio Della Favorita between the other two teams in our group, Holland and Egypt.

The Dutch, who had knocked us out of the European Championships and gone on to win the title, were hot favourites to finish top of our group. They were also being tipped to go all the way and win the World Cup. Their team hadn't changed too much over the previous two years and still included world-class players like Marco Van Basten, Frank Rijkaard and Ruud Gullit. That night they were lucky to escape with a point in a 1-1 draw with the Egyptians, who at times played them off the park with their free-flowing football.

Egypt had been the underdogs in the group. They were there supposedly to make the numbers. But their draw with Holland meant that we were all back to square one in Group F. We had all played a game, scored a goal, conceded a goal and had a point each. Jack was surprised at what he had seen. He never underestimates the opposition, but the Egyptians had played so well that now England and ourselves would have to treat them with the utmost respect. It was early curtains that night. Many of the lads were still a bit tired from the previous evening's celebrations. So it was off to grab some shut-eye with a helicopter whirring around the room!

The training ground at Terrasini was beautiful. The surface was great, with the mountains providing a scenic backdrop. Preparation for the match against Egypt began in earnest on Wednesday with many of our fans sitting in the stands at Terrasini. With all the hard graft already done in Malta, all we would do was a few stretching exercises and then play a five-a-side.

After training on Thursday Jack allowed us to go into Palermo for a few hours in the afternoon. 'No drink,' he warned. I met Fiona there with Woody (Mike Wood) a mate of mine from Wilmslow in Cheshire – and again there was more trouble. Fiona seemed to be jinxed in Italy. They had hired a car. I met them in town and we went for a walk around to buy some souvenirs. Every place was closed for the afternoon – I'm sure Jack, God love him, knew that. We ended up having some coffee in a café and then I left them back to the car. But it was gone. Maybe it was a different street? Maybe it had been pinched? We went back to the coach and one of the Italia'90 officials agreed to make some enquiries. They finally tracked it down to a car pound. Nice one, Woody and Fiona.

We had been away so long now and because we were confined to barracks outside of training time passed very slowly. There were the usual card schools, and the few thrillers in English that had been brought out by some of the more enterprising players were well thumbed by now. That and the World Cup matches that were on television most nights. It's then that you look forward to meal times and other such things that you usually take for granted – and then every night it was back upstairs to the dreaded whirlybirds!

We trained on Saturday and then Jack told us that the team would be unchanged, the same that had played against England. There was still no place for Ronnie Whelan although he appeared to be fit. Ronnie would have been a certain starter in Italy but for an unfortunate injury near the end of the season with Liverpool. He had broken a bone in his foot, but it didn't go into plaster until a week after the accident. So he had missed a few games and couldn't train very hard in Turkey or Malta. He had begun to get back into the run of things in Sardinia, but Jack was still afraid the injury might not have healed enough to be able to throw him in at the deep end. Ronnie's a naturally fit person – but Jack was still afraid to take a chance. Even though all twenty-two players in the squad were like a family, if you weren't playing or named among the substitutes you felt left out of the whole thing. It was hard for some of the lads, but Jack could pick only one team – and five substitutes.

On Saturday evening England played Holland in Cagliari. They played with a sweeper, Mark Wright, behind central defenders Terry Butcher and Des Walker, and confused the Dutch with their tactics. It was unheard of. The Continental teams always play a sweeper while the British style is a flat back four. Wright played brilliantly and England found the net twice – only for the referee to overrule them. A team had still to win a game in our group. We would go top if we beat Egypt the following afternoon in Palermo.

IRELAND / EGYPT MATCH

We went into that game with high expectations, as did our fans. We didn't think there were any worries about losing it. Jack was confident in the dressingroom too. Just do our job and everything would be all right.

But the Egyptians changed their tactics. They made sure they had every man behind the ball when we attacked. We bombarded them up to half-time and got nowhere. Jack told us to up our game in the second-half. We did – but still nothing. A little bit of craft or guile might have opened them up, but the Egyptians stuck to their job. They used every trick in the book to make sure they kept us out. They wasted so much time, their goalkeeper took ages at his kick-outs and when the ball ran out of play they sauntered over to collect it and then proceeded to ask the referee what it was, a throw-in or free kick? They frustrated us. But we should have been able to break them down. It ended 0-0. Nothing had changed in the group. Every team's record was the same: played 2, drew 2, 1 goal for, 1 goal against, and we all had two points each. The difference now was that we would meet Holland in our final match while England had the Egyptians. All of a sudden we seemed to be staring elimination in the face.

As we came off the field I looked up at our supporters and felt so guilty. We should have beaten the Egyptians. The dressingroom was like a morgue. Every player was gutted and we found it hard to lift each other. We had to get a result now against the Dutch or we were out, on the way home. It was Tony Cascarino who summed it up best when he said that the team felt so low at that moment we could have all parachuted out of a snake's arse.

Jack was livid. He was disappointed with the way we had played, but he was angry at the Egyptians' approach to the game. He told a post-match press conference how he felt. One Egyptian said that their team hadn't come to play us. Jack really slaughtered him. We had come to play, we had tried to win a game and they were out there just to be negative. 'We don't let other teams play in our half of the field but by Christ we try and play in their half. We don't sit back, we attack,' Jack insisted. I spoke to Jack afterwards and he felt what he said was going to sound like sour grapes. But it wasn't. That was how he felt. He's honest and he went in there and spoke from the heart.

The Italian media had by now dubbed Group F *'El Grupo Morte'* – the dead group. I don't know about that but it was certainly sudden death now. Only two teams had beaten us in competitive games since June 1988 – Spain and Holland. But all was not well in the Dutch camp. Stories came back to us about trouble between manager Leo Beenhakker and some of his most important players. There was even talk of them bringing in a psychoanalyst to see if he could do something to sort out their problems. We already had one – Big Jack!

It was back to training the following day, Monday. Back to the same routine, but the Dutch match lay heavy on our minds. Then in training on Tuesday Jack decided to play three across the back – Kevin Moran, David O'Leary and myself. We played against the lads who hadn't figured in any of the games yet and they hammered us. I didn't like the idea of playing the three of us but I went along with it. Jack had seen the English frustrate the Dutch with that system and for one minute he might have thought of trying the same tactic himself. But our 'reserves' took us apart and he dropped the idea.

Cas missed a few chances that day too. So in the second half of the practice game Jack tells Cas to swop shirts with Niall Quinn who was a substitute. 'If anyone ask you why I'm doing it just tell them you missed two chances in the first half and you were crap,' Jack says to Cas. That's the way he talks to us. He doesn't mean any harm and we all get a laugh out of it. Nobody thought Cas wouldn't be playing against the Dutch. I told him that Jack had just done it to wind up the media who were watching the knockabout. Jack changed things around again and put Kevin and myself back into the centre and we began to play a little better. The other system had failed. The three of us were getting dragged all over the place because we didn't know who was playing where. Later Jack announced his team. Cas had been dropped and Niall was in against the Dutch. Cas was bitterly disappointed.

IRELAND / HOLLAND MATCH

On the way to the stadium in the bus on Thursday evening Cas was still devastated. He had played in every World Cup qualifying game and our first two in Italy and now he found himself on the outside. I tried to console him, which is easy when you're playing. If I had been dropped nobody in the world could have consoled me. What made it worse was that Cas asked me if I could get Gullit's shirt for him after the match. But I had already got one from Gullit when we played in the European Championships and I wanted to try for a different one. Cas said to me, 'you'll pull a fast one and get Van Basten's and then you won't give it to me.' To keep him quiet I agreed to ask Gullit.

The dressingroom was very tense. Jack emphasised that the Dutch hadn't played well and that if they went into the match with the same arrogant swagger as they did against the Egyptians then they would soon be in trouble. But we all knew they wouldn't. This game was make or break for both us. And we had ruffled their feathers in Germany, so they would treat us with a little more respect this time.

Then Jack started talking about some of their players. He talked about Van Cleef and Cuelemans. I told him that Van Cleef was a movie star and that Cuelemans played for Belgium! He meant Wim Kieft and Koeman. But that broke the ice a little and everyone had a little laugh at his expense. We walked out on the pitch and the noise was deafening. The last time we had played the Dutch the stadium in Gelsenkirchen was smothered in orange. It looked as if the Dutch fans had got their hands on every ticket for that match. It was different this time – there was just as much green. Of course I lost the toss again and as I shook Gullit's hand before the kick-off I asked him could we exchange shirts after the game, and he agreed. As I walked back to take up my position, I felt really nervous and I could sense that the rest of the lads felt the same.

The Dutch started well, knocking the ball about like we knew they could. We were getting pushed back and I think all of us thought — Oh no, here we go. This was a different team to the one that was lucky to draw with Egypt and lucky not to get beaten by England. This was not the script we had read before the game. Yet we were managing to hold them. All their good football was being played in front of our defence but they were not penetrating it.

Then they scored. A wonderful one-two between Gullit and Kieft at the edge of the box and Gullit is in and gives Packie no chance with his shot. It's then that you can get the feeling, here we go, they've got one. But in reality you roll up your sleeves and say to yourself: Right, you sods, we're going to have a go.

ONE DOWN AT HALF-TIME

We needed just one goal to stay in the competition and we set out to get it. The lads responded magnificently. Aldo had what looked like a perfectly good goal disallowed. Then we had a penalty turned down when Niall Quinn was flattened in the box. We were beginning to frustrate them. They were finding it extremely hard to contain us and we forced them back. They had to work overtime to keep us at bay. We went in at half-time and Jack had a go at us about the goal we had given away. It was a great finish but the way it had been conceded had upset him. But he was pleased with our attitude after they had scored. We had begun to play and they were scared of us. If we just kept going at them then the goal would come. Jack was convinced of that.

THE SECOND HALF

Back out for the second-half and we started where we left off. It was whirlwind pace, up and at them all the time. As those precious minutes passed we pushed more and more players forward and on a couple of occasions they might have caught us on the break.

Then our goal came. Packie launched the ball up the field and it landed on their right back's foot. He couldn't control it properly and all he could do was try and hit it back to Van Breukelen in goal. Van Breukelen wasn't ready for that and the ball rolled away from him. Niall was on it in double-quick time and slid it home, 1-1. Now we're pushing forward looking for the winner – but we also know that one slip at our end and we were out.

One of our lads went down with a knock and as Mick Byrne came on to give him treatment he told me that England were winning 1-0 against Egypt in Cagliari. If the scores remained the same in both games then England, Holland and Ireland would be through to the last sixteen of the competition.

I saw Gullit and told him the score. He knew what had to be done – but just in case he didn't I made sure he realised that we had taken control of the game! We could battle it out for the remaining fifteen minutes. If we did go at it then the odds were stacked against Holland. We didn't agree on any plan, but as soon as the game re-started Gullit went back into defence and started to knock the ball about there. Then when the ball was kicked up to us we played around with it and sent it back down to them. What we were doing was probably too obvious so the referee called Gullit and myself over to him. He had already had words with me about some of the lads who kept letting their shirts hang over their knicks. He talked to me in French and obviously thought I knew the language from my days with Olympique Lyon. He had been picky about the shirts. But I just explained to him that players like Niall Quinn were so big it was hard to get shirts to fit them. That's why Quinny was having trouble keeping his shirt stuck down his knicks! Niall looked like a belly dancer and Paul McGrath was having problems with his shirt as well. This time, however, the referee wanted Gullit and myself to explain ourselves and he told us that we must play football. I said, 'Listen this IS the first time we've had a chance to play football, the first time we've knocked two passes together for four years – and you want us to stop!' He understood – and we just got on with the game.

The ball was just being batted forward and back again but Van Basten was still very busy, I don't think he had realised what he was supposed to do. The rest of his team were playing to 'plan'. I told him that if he continued the way he was playing he would get a rocket – from his own team! Van Basten usually keeps out of the fray when the game gets a little physical. But now, with both teams strolling about, he's getting very busy in our area. I had to tell him the script.

But the same thing is happening up the other end of the field. Quinner and Tony Cascarino, who had come on for Aldo, hadn't copped on. (Ronald Koeman, the talented Dutch central defender who plays for Barcelona, told me that when we met in Portugal after we were both eliminated from the World Cup finals. Koeman was there with his family on holiday and so was I. We watched the final together and he told me how every time the ball was pumped forward, Niall and Cas were knocking hell out of their defence. Fortunately they found out in time that a point from that game was good enough for us.) Finally the clock ran out and we were through with Holland. Little did we know at the time that Egypt missed a glaring chance close to the end of their clash with England that would have left all four teams in the group with identical records. Then it would have been a real lottery. We would all have had to go into a hat and draw lots!

IN THE LAST SIXTEEN

We had made it. We were in the last sixteen. England had finished top of the group with four points and they would go on to meet Belgium in the next round. While we were celebrating in the dressingroom later, Holland and ourselves went into a draw in Rome to see who would meet West Germany in one last sixteen match and Romania in the other. At last we had a little luck and drew the Romanians in Genoa five days later.

As the celebrations began on the pitch, Gullit, remembering the promise he had made to me before kick-off, came up the field to exchange shirts. But Quinny grabbed him and tried to do a swap. Gullit told him, 'No way – this is for your captain.' I was dead chuffed about that. Quinny stood there agog with his mouth open. He didn't know it had already been arranged. But Niall's reason for getting Gullit's shirt was a selfless one. Gary Waddock had asked him to try and get that particular shirt as a momento of the World Cup finals and Niall had tried to keep the promise. I told Niall that we would sort it out with Cas after the match – now, on the field, it was celebration time.

CELEBRATIONS

We had proved a lot of people wrong. We had made it to the last sixteen of the World Cup finals and everybody was so proud and excited. It was great on the park. We saluted the fans, they saluted us and the message to them was: See you in Genoa in a few days. Jack was happy, to say the least. The pressure was off us all.

For the players the result was that bit extra special because our wives had been there. We had wanted them for that match, we wanted to share our success with them. After all, they were the most important people to us, the ones who had stuck by us through thick and thin. And Jack agreed to let them come back so we could celebrate with them. So when we got back to the hotel they were all there – except Fiona. The Italian jinx had struck again. She had got lost with a couple of mates of mine on the way to the hotel and missed the turn-off for the team's headquarters. Lost yet again.

When I got into the hotel the celebrations had begun. There were kisses and congratulations all around from the wives. I got a bottle of beer and headed up to my room. There was a wonderful smell of perfume in the corridor. It was beautiful. Having spent the previous three weeks with twenty-one sweaty, smelly players, it was like a breath of fresh air. When Fiona turned up a little later I told her about the smell. It's one of those little things that will stay with me as part of my World Cup memories.

We arranged to meet Frank Stapleton, my roommate, and his wife, Chris, downstairs later. Frank had booked into a separate room so that Fiona and I could spend some time together. Fiona had a bath, I had a bath and we got changed – and then we just sat there on the bed and chatted for what seemed like hours. We talked about the kids, whom I missed a lot, and just silly things about houses in Kent where we were thinking of moving after the transfer to Millwall. Just private family things.

But when we came down, some of the lads were giving us that nudge nudge, wink wink bit. I was much too knackered for anything like that! All Fiona and I wanted to do was have a chat. It was a wonderful night. We sat down with Frank and Chris, Jack and his wife, Pat, and had the crack. It was one of the highlights of the trip. We had a great sing-song and Larry Mullen from U2 was there, mixing with the lads. We had a few drinks, but had to remember we were leaving again early the following morning. Still I didn't get to my room with Fiona until after three o'clock.

I was physically so tired after the match, but the mental buzz kept me awake. I didn't get too much sleep with the helicopter in the room. Fiona, on the other hand, hit the pillow and was out cold in minutes. I would doze on and off for fifteen or twenty minutes at a time and then would wake up again.

By 6am I couldn't stand it any more. I got up and went down to see if I could try and get a cup of tea. Kevin Moran was already there. He couldn't sleep either. He had a toothache. We went for a swim at about 6.30am. We were making a lot of noise. But we were up, so why shouldn't the rest of the lads rise and shine too? The celebrations were well and truly over and now it was time to get packed and move on to Genoa.

GENOA

GENOA WAS SOMETHING SPECIAL. The Bristol hotel, in a district called Rapallo, was magnificent, the rooms were big with a wonderful view overlooking the Med – and the food was brilliant, excellent quality and plenty of it! The lads joked about that. Now that we had found a place where they could look after us, there was no need for Eddie Corcoran any more. It was: 'Go home, Eddie, you're redundant.' The hotel had already experienced the World Cup, as the Scottish team had stayed there before being eliminated from the competition. We arrived around noon on Friday, June 22. We were tired, so there was no training.

On Saturday morning some of us trained. There were a few injuries and other players were still trying to recover from the Dutch match – and the post-game celebrations. We did nothing spectacular. Jack and Maurice Setters just watched as we did some crossing and shooting. However, I did end up with the yellow jersey for bad performance! I got it not for being the worst player in training, but the grumpiest. We were beaten 4-3 in the knockabout. These games are meant to be what their name suggests, a friendly five-a-side. But I hate being beaten even at that level so when we were finished I knocked over the water and kicked the bollards on the pitch. I calmed down only when I went into goal and two local kids took shots at me for a few minutes.

On the way back on the bus John Sheridan collected the yellow jersey votes. It was a three-way split between Alan McLoughlin, Dave O'Leary and myself. There was a second round of votes and Alan was left out. I 'won' the final vote and earned the jersey. Needless to say I took it with my usual dignity and snarled at everybody. Besides all that, however, it had been a fun session.

Later that afternoon Jack took us into Rapallo for a walkabout. It was meant just to get us out of the hotel so we wouldn't get too bored. As we got off the coach in the town Jack gave us our orders: No booze and, because of the heat, we were to wear hats so that the sun wouldn't burn us, or frazzle our brains. Anybody caught without a hat would be fined £10. We just walked around and I remember buying some tee-shirts. Then five or six of us ordered some coffees at a café and sat outside and relaxed. We had just about started the coffees when Jack came around the corner with Mick Byrne and Charlie O'Leary in tow. He looked over at us and began to count: 'That's 10, 20, 30, 40, 50, 60 quid – none of you are wearing hats!' After another little stroll it was back on the bus and off to the hotel. I remember that evening well. We stuffed ourselves with all this great food and then headed off to bed early. I was looking forward to going to bed that evening, knowing that there wouldn't be a helicopter in my room!

TRAINING SESSIONS

On Sunday, the day before the match, we went down to have a workout at the Stadio Luigi Ferraris ground. It struck me as one of the most unusual I have ever seen. The huge columns at each corner of the ground reminded me of a multi-storey car park where drivers get back to the street by walking down through those turrets. It's the home of Sampdoria, one of the teams that Liam Brady played for when he was in Italy. Having said that, the stadium was still a hell of a lot better than a lot of those in Britain. We arrived there at about 11am and it was already stifling. We were worried about the heat for the following afternoon when the game was due to kick off at 4pm.

I decided not to take part. I wasn't injured – maybe I had a broken nail or twisted my eyelash! – just still a little tired. It had all caught up with me by now. I just sat there and watched the rest of the lads go through their paces. We still had injuries, and a couple of the others also felt like me and sat it out. So, of course, without me the little match at the end of the session is a friendly one, not too many rash words or tackles going in – plain boring actually! I'm sure the Italians watching couldn't believe it was an international football team.

Back on the bus it's voting time again for the bad performance jersey. Jack is doing his usual thing – trying to make sure that Kevin Sheedy wins it. Jack has this theory why Sheedy never wins the damned jersey. It's because nobody ever sees him kick a ball during training! Jack didn't get his way though; the vote was between Paul McGrath, Frank Stapleton and Ray Houghton. They're all strange faces when it comes to the vote. But John Byrne made a late run and he won the jersey that morning.

THE NIGHT BEFORE THE MATCH

Back at the hotel Jack announces that after dinner we would watch some video tapes of the earlier Romanian games. I hate that. I hate watching the other teams. It gets me thinking about the game and I don't like doing that until the last few hours before kick-off. Jack wanted to watch an hour of one game and an hour of another. I just hated the thought of it. We had a snooze in the afternoon and then came down for dinner at around 5pm – and then to watch the tapes. But as luck would have it the Brazil versus Argentina match was on television and everybody wanted to watch that. There were about sixty people in the lounge, many sitting on the floor, watching the game. Some of the lads sloped off to play snooker, pool or the pinball machines. And Jack was moaning: 'It's great to see you all so interested in our game tomorrow.'

When the game was finished Jack brought his tapes out. That was it. I disappeared. Jack was mad. 'Bloody hell, nice to see you are all so interested in what you're doing. You have got Romania tomorrow and you won't watch the tapes.' So a lot of the lads sat there for an hour and watched the first tape and were bored to death. Then it was off for the highlight of the day – another great meal in the Bristol. We made absolute pigs of ourselves – again – and then it was back in for another video horror. This time most of us watched some of it, to see how they play and to watch what they do at corner kicks and free kicks.

It's important to get a good night's sleep before a match. But the lads were a bit reluctant to head for their rooms. Some of them were talking – maybe a bit of nerves to be seen – some playing cards, a few outside having a coffee, having a chat, and some had gone for a stroll around the hotel. But nobody was doing anything in particular. We were all trying to take our minds off the game. If you were asked were you doing it on purpose, you would probably say No. It's all a bit subconscious, you just do it.

The following morning I got up early and had my usual swim, then breakfasted with the early risers. Some of the others didn't get up for breakfast, but just came down in time for lunch. I sat in the breakfast room with some of the team and drank tea and then went out on the verandah and had a chat with a few more of the players. We had a light lunch at noon, then a hour or so in bed and by about 2.30pm we are ready to head for the stadium. On the coach the music goes on to get the lads wound up. As we hit Genoa we begin to see the green, white and gold of the Irish tricolour. It's everywhere. The fans are cheering us in the streets and the atmosphere is beginning to build. There are thousands of fans outside the ground making their way in. It's a fabulous scene. We go into the dressingroom, drop our kit and then go out onto the pitch just to check the surface. It's stifling – 3.30pm in the afternoon and the sun is right above the ground. There is no breeze at all. If there was it wouldn't get into that ground, it's totally sealed off.

IRELAND / ROMANIA MATCH

The heat is incredible and the atmosphere is unbelievable. Half of Ireland must have made the trip. There are Irish flags everywhere. They outnumber the Romanian ones ten to one at least. And it's party time for the fans. They're singing their hearts out and the match hasn't even kicked off yet.

We were there very early for that game. Jack was concerned that we shouldn't get ready too soon and burn off too much energy in the sun while warming up. He told us when we came back in to sit down, relax, put our feet up and, if we wanted, to have a cold shower. We were going to need all our energy in that heat.

A couple of the team – Ronnie and goalkeeper Gerry Peyton – went out for a kickabout because they weren't playing. Ronnie said to Gerry: 'Come on out and I'll blast the ball at you in the goal, and ruin your confidence.' So Ronnie goes out with Gerry and takes penalties, free kicks, generally whacks the ball at Gerry – and ruins his confidence! The rest of us sit in the dressingroom trying to relax. But the nerves are there – everyone visits the toilet at least once. Jacks tells us to drink as much water as possible, without feeling ill because you get dehydrated out there very quickly.

Now the last-minute preparations are going on. Somebody's strapping is too tight – Can I have it loosened? Where's me pads? Charlie, have you got the polish? Let me clean me boots. Have you got any chewing gum? Where's the tie-ups? Somebody can't find water. It's just a little tension, that's all. Then there is always somebody trying to break the ice. Ronnie is trying to keep the ball up in the air in the dressingroom, or smashing it against the wall. Then he hits something or somebody on the head and everybody has a laugh. The ice is broken.

Jack began to go around among the players. He told us all to keep it tight at the back and Packie to sweep up behind us for the ball over the top, get the ball into the channels. He was going through the basics of the way he wants us to play – and keep it tight. This is it. If we win this we are off to Rome to play Italy, so it is big time stuff, we are ready for the off.

ON THE PITCH

The roar when we went out onto the pitch was deafening. It was like playing at Lansdowne, it was that noisy. I tossed the coin and, you guessed it, I lost again. I know I lost because Packie wanted to play the other way in the first-half. Packie was annoyed with me – again! – and now you know why I don't gamble.

But we had the ball and we kicked off. It was the same story all over again. Like the Dutch, the Romanians had us on the rack for the first fifteen minutes or so. They were brilliant and really had us under the cosh. But then they gradually began to slow up a little and we started to inflict our game on them. They were backing off so much that instead of Packie playing the ball up-field, Kevin, Chris Morris, Steve Staunton and myself were finding our lads up-front. But when the Romanians came forward they were sharp, quick and had bags of skill. I'm told that I ended the tournament with the most number of fouls and I think I got away with murder in that game in those early exchanges. I had a piggy-back off their centre forward, a right tussle with Gheorge Hagi, a run-in with almost every one of their players in the first forty-five minutes. But it was all straight up-front, there was no nastiness, rolling about, no tackling from behind or anything like that.

HALF-TIME

Half-time couldn't come soon enough. The heat had been unbelievable. I couldn't stop sweating. I was pouring water in and it was coming straight out of me. I felt as if I had wet myself. I was so wet it was incredible – everyone was the same. We sat there, relaxed, got the pads off, legs up in the air, sat against a cold wall, anything to try and cool down. We all had wet towels around our heads.

Jack was delighted with us. He liked the way we took the initiative and started playing out of the back, knocking balls into Quinny and Cas up-front. He was really pleased with the way things were going. All he can say is that maybe we just need a little bit more, a little bit of luck to start with. We had a few chances – maybe a little bit more composure when we get into positions to put the final ball in or have a shot.

SECOND HALF

We started very much the same way in the second half. The ball comes back to me at the edge of the box, and it's off again, up and at them. By now, even though we have another forty-five minutes to play, the heat is beginning to take its toll. But Hagi is still very busy, he's playing very well. He's taking on our lads and beating them for the fun of it. But his final pass, his final shot lets him down.

Packie pulled off a couple of great saves. He had an exceptional game actually. The Romanians didn't have a lot of chances. They had a few long-range shots that Packie had to deal with and he dealt with them in his usual way – cool, calm and collected. Niall had a couple of chances and Cas had a fine header. He rose above everybody to knock it down and their goalkeeper made a great save on the line. The last ten or fifteen minutes just drifted away. Fatigue under the blazing sun was setting in fast. But that affected both teams. All twenty-two players on the pitch were on the verge of collapse. Then the whistle went 0-0 – another thirty minutes of torture lay ahead.

The pace had dropped dramatically by now and there was precious little football played. Both teams were only too well aware that one mistake in this heat and it was all over. We also knew that one inspired moment of magic could end it. I was nervous about that and I told all the players that we weren't to take any chances, especially at the back. A penalty shootout is looming. Ironically I think both teams were quite calm about that. It would have been dreadful to blow it in extra time. The penalties seemed to be a better way to decide the game. I was personally glad it was going to penalties because in the last minute the ball was played into one of the corners. I chased out to get it and I got this terrible surge of rising damp (cramp!) in my legs.

PENALTY SHOOT-OUT

By the time I hauled myself over to the bench for a drink they had decided who would take the penalties. I certainly didn't want to take one of them. I couldn't live with myself if I was the one that missed a penalty which put the Republic out of the World Cup finals. Dave O'Leary said he would take one, but he wanted to go last. That was a very brave decision. Dave had come on for Steve Staunton who had been injured and had just played his first thirty minutes of the World Cup finals. Andy Townsend, Ray Houghton and Kevin Sheedy also volunteered. Cas didn't fancy one but the lads convinced him. He took them in training and always did well.

I went around to all the lads, especially the penalty-takers, and said that whatever happened now we had had a great tournament. We had done better than most people had expected. We had not disgraced ourselves. The players entrusted with the penalties were told not to worry about it, just go and take your kick. Just do your best. No matter what happens we will have a drink tonight and celebrate. If we are eliminated then we will just go home and reflect on what we have done rather than what might have been.

Jack did the same, told all the lads just to do their best. Then the rest of the team shook hands with those taking the penalties. There was solidarity with them. That was one of the main reasons we had travelled so far together. It was very much one for all and all for one.

We all had to remain in the centre circle for the penalties and the referee came over and told us to pull our socks up and get our shin pads in. I couldn't believe it. We had just played over two hours in a scorching sun and the referee wants us to get dressed! 'What for?' I asked – I'm not taking a penalty, my game is over … bollocks to it. The referee said we must all remain properly dressed while on the field. I pulled them up. He hadn't made the rules. By the time he had said all this to me and I had my few words, it was time for the penalties to be taken. It was time for another bloody toss to see who went first and I lost again. I wanted to win that one more than anything. If you go first and score then it puts pressure on the other team to score, to equalise. We would now have to play catch-up. This was the first time a game had gone to penalties in the finals.

Every time we scored, the lads were elated – every time they scored we were pissed off. They scored, then we equalised. It went like that right up to the last two kicks. Then Packie does it. He makes a brilliant save from Timofte. We will be through to the last eight in the finals if Dave can convert the final penalty. He has only been on the field for thirty minutes and he steps up and sends the goalkeeper the wrong way. It's 5-4 on penalties to the Republic.

The cramp and fatigue were forgotten as we ran to greet Packie and Dave. The scene inside the stadium was incredible. Total joy, total elation. We could have stayed on the park all night just standing waving to the fans and listening to them. But we had a party to get to that night – the biggest Genoa has ever seen.

Still, I felt for the Romanians. I went round and shook hands with them, swopped a jersey with them – you always do that; you see them trudging off, and it could be you. It takes just a couple of minutes to shake their hands. We went around and applauded the crowd again. As always, they were wonderful.

IN THE DRESSINGROOM

In the dressingroom afterwards I think everyone had a little cry. There were a few who broke down, they were so physically and emotionally drained. A lot of tears were shed because we were all so happy. It was all done openly and honestly. Then we came back down to earth with a bump – and anybody caught crying had the piss taken out of him.

Then there are little jobs to be done. The body has taken a pummelling and there's ice flying about to go on knees and ankles. Hamstrings are seen to, all types of strains are looked at. Then the search for a beer begins and when that's sorted out it's time to catch the coach back to the hotel.

Outside, the media had gathered asking us how we will cope with Italy in the quarter-finals. An interesting question considering that Italy had still to play Uruguay that evening for the right to meet us in the quarter-finals. Playing Italy in Rome is what everyone wanted.

We might stand a better chance against Uruguay, but then again if we beat Italy in front of their fanatical fans in Rome's Olympic stadium we might just be setting ourselves up to go all the way. All the Italian media however are quite sure it will be Italy in the last eight. I told them that they shouldn't count their chickens before they have hatched – and then I spent the next five minutes trying to explain to them what that quaint English expression meant!

CELEBRATIONS

I sat at the front of the coach on the way back to the hotel. We were all looking forward to the night's celebrations. I don't know how the others felt, but I certainly felt a great sense of relief. Then those famous tapes go on and everybody is singing all the way through Genoa and out into Rapallo. There is already a crowd at the hotel and everybody wants to shake your hand and pat you on the back.

Once again, most of our wives were going to join us for the evening. We showered, changed quickly and within thirty minutes we were back down for dinner. It was a real family occasion. Some of the players' parents, brothers, sisters, cousins etc had joined us by now. The crack was great as we waited for the result of the Italy-Uruguay match. Then the news came through. Italy had beaten them 2-0 and we would meet them in Rome the following Saturday evening. We did some radio and newspaper interviews and an RTE TV link-up to Dublin which was fun. Then it was time to head out for the night. We would have the usual early flight in the morning but right then all we wanted to do was go out and paint the town green.

ROME

THE FOLLOWING MORNING WE WERE OFF AGAIN. But this time we had our families with us. It was chaos down in the hotel lobby, absolute bedlam. The party had swelled to well over sixty by now because the FAI officials had joined us. We were due to leave the hotel at a designated time and it was then postponed an hour because of the chaos. The real problem was our luggage – would it arrive in Rome at the same time as us – or a day later. It was manic, and we finally left with just our personal belongings like wallets, passports and money. We got to the airport and it was chaotic there too. There were bags and cases everywhere, but we managed to get everything on to the plane and we were finally up, up and away to Rome.

It had already turned into a nightmare of a day with all the confusion. For the players it was just another trip and you tend to get brassed off with all the travel after a while. People think it's glamorous, but for the players the 'glamour' and crack comes after the games when we can get out for the night. All the bits in between – the packing, the unpacking, flying here, flying there – it can get to you after a while.

When we got to Rome airport we had to sit around for about an hour waiting for our luggage. Uruguay were flying out at the same time, returning home having been beaten by Italy the previous evening. Then there was the welcoming committee and a speech from one of the officials. So after what seemed like ages we were finally on the last leg of our journey to our hotel. It was now early afternoon and we were starving.

As soon as we got there it was straight into the restaurant for a meal with our wives and FAI officials. The food was basic, very basic. The steak was fairly tough, and there wasn't too much of it either. Not too many vegetables, followed by some ice cream and a cup of coffee. After the Hotel Bristol, this was positively minor league. The lads were far from pleased. Immediately after the meal we said goodbye to our wives and relatives who were heading off to another hotel. We stood in reception getting allocated our rooms and there were little rumblings about the hotel. It really didn't look that appealing at all.

It's now that the little arguments can start. But they normally don't with our gang. They're such a great bunch that it takes a lot to get them going.

We were allocated our rooms and some of the lads have already headed up. But five minutes later they are back down, fuming. 'You should see the rooms, the size of them, you couldn't swing a cat in them – two beds stuck in a single room,' was the cleanest comment. As captain I get pulled out by the others and I go and see Jack. But Jack is cute enough, he has seen what is happening already and before I could even get to him he is on his way out to find out what the problem is. I explain our situation to him. 'The lads are far from happy, Jack. The rooms are minute. We have been away for four weeks and we have got three or four cases each, bags full of stuff and it's a single room with two single beds in,' I tell him. 'You couldn't put a needle down without it being in somebody's way.' What was even more frustrating for us was that there *were* double rooms but they had been occupied already by people who weren't playing.

Jack had a big room. He is the manager after all, but to be fair to him, he was the first one to come down and say: 'Look lads, I've got a big room. I've not got much gear, you can have my room.' Maurice Setters, Jack's assistant was the same. So eventually somebody got Jack's room and I got Maurice's. The FAI officials had to leave their bigger rooms, they had to accommodate the players. They had to up and leave and go to another hotel. So that was the start, another mess-up. We are here to play in what is the most important game in Ireland's history and we have got off to a bad start.

But the lads being the lads soon got over the hassles and began to focus their minds on the job in hand. Then the hotel telephone lines were buzzing with calls from our wives. Their hotel is a dump, ten times worse than the one we're in! Things were going from bad to worse. However, the following day the girls, in solidarity with each other, walked out and found another hotel nearer to Rome's centre. It was a big improvement and of course it left them nearer to all the big fashion houses. Some of the lads are still paying the bills for that one! We didn't do a lot that day. There was no training. Eddie was back on the job of sorting out the kitchens! We were all very tired and for most of us it was an early night.

THE VISIT TO THE POPE

ON TUESDAY, OUR SECOND DAY IN ROME, we resumed training. But the session was overshadowed by rumours that we might have an audience with the Pope. All the talk the night before was that somebody was trying to set it up. Jack had always said to Mick Byrne and Charlie O'Leary that he would get us to Rome, and once there HE would get us an audience with the Pope. We all still thought it was a bit of pie in the sky. But when we came back from training that day we were told it was on. We were off to the Vatican the following morning.

We were all up early that day – including Paul McGrath! It was great, everybody was going, the players, their wives and the FAI officers. It was astonishing that morning. We had all been told to wear our white tracksuits for the visit. Usually on an occasion like this when we're going to a reception, there's always one person who forgets and wears something different. That morning, however, everybody had on the same kit. Wonderful.

And then the jokes start on the bus, and they're all aimed at poor Mick Byrne. Mick is deeply religious, a devout Catholic. Everyone is trying to get a rise out of him. One of the lads turns and asks Mick: does he think the Pope was out for a pint the previous evening? Then it starts big time. Will he have a hangover? Will he be up to seeing us? It was just some gentle ribbing to pass the time on the bus.

Now we were in St Peter's Square. We were dropped off and the first thing that hit me was the heat, and then the supporters. There were hundreds of them there just to soak up the history and pay a visit to one of the most beautiful buildings in the world.

We gathered ourselves together and made our way through the square. Our leader was Monsignor Liam Boyle, a wonderful man. It was his influence that made our visit possible. I think he was as proud as punch as well. We were ushered quickly into a huge, magnificent room, which was surprisingly modern. Thousands of people were already sitting there. The place was truly immense, and we were led up to the front and seated to the right of the podium where the Pope would sit. Our wives, the officials and the Irish press corps were given seats too. Finally the Pope made his entrance. It was unbelievable, just to be in the same room as the man, even though there were 10,000 seats in the place and every one was full. And we were less than thirty yards away from him. I can't describe the feeling. I just felt very lucky, very privileged and honoured to be in there.

He made his speech in English, then in all the other languages. I think he spoke in German next and when he was finished I applauded him. And Jack nudged me and asked, 'Why are you applauding, you didn't understand a word he said!' But I was totally immersed in the whole thing. It might never happen to me again so I was going to enjoy every moment of it. Anyway, it was just polite to applaud him. But the lads were becoming a little restless now, the ceremony had been going on for quite some time. We had been sitting on these very hard, school-like chairs and you could hear the fidgeting behind, hamstrings acting up from the Romanian game, and different little knocks starting to irritate.

Finally, one of the Pope's officials came across and told Jack that we could go and stand in the middle of the podium. His Holiness wanted to meet us, and we could have a picture taken with him. Normally the lads are a bit reserved about things like that. But this was the Pope in the Vatican, so there was a tremendous scramble for positions. I wasn't too worried because I knew that Mick Byrne and myself would be making presentations to him. I was to give him a shirt signed by the whole squad. I was delighted, but also a little bit embarrassed. I was also very honoured because the shirt was one of mine.

The Pope came over and he wanted to meet Packie. Mind you, at that stage everybody wanted to shake hands with the big fella after his penalty save against Romania. But His Holiness wanted to meet him because as a young lad living in Poland he had been a goalkeeper too. Then he just got in the middle of us and threw his arm around Charlie O'Leary. It was all so spontaneous and wonderful as we stood there for a special photograph. He was there for a couple of minutes and we knew he had so many more people to meet, so an official came over to me and told me to present him with the shirt now. I walked to His Holiness, gave him the shirt, kissed his ring and shook his hand. It was all over in a few seconds, but I will never forget it.

PREPARING TO PLAY ITALY

We were all still on a high that afternoon as we resumed serious training for the match against Italy. Meeting the Pope was a marvellous moment, a wonderful occasion. But now the match is just seventy-two hours away – the biggest match of our lives. The training ground was about two minutes from the hotel by coach. When we arrived there were plenty of people around – media, fans, and the Opel wolfhound. This fella had been sent by the Irish team's major sponsors, Opel, to be the mascot in Italy. So he followed us around, mixing with the fans, dressed up in this big, heavy costume as an Irish wolfhound. The poor lad, he started off a fine strapping fellow, but now he must have been down to about nine-and-a-half stone with the heat. When I think back to the stifling heat in Genoa, we suffered nothing compared to what he put up with inside that dog suit! Now the temperatures were shooting up in Rome. They would reach around 95 degrees in the afternoon.

Training never changes. We do some loosening-up exercises then play a five-a-side. We are just ticking over now. It's much too late to think about doing anything strenuous. Our bodies are finely tuned from the two weeks in Malta. Jack doesn't put any pressure on the players to train. Those with little knocks take a back seat at the sessions. They join the rest of the squad on the benches and slag off the rest of us during the five-a-side. And at last Kevin Sheedy wins the yellow jersey!

Back at the hotel in the evening it's the same old drudgery. With the match less than seventy-two hours away there's no chance of stepping out. The heat is such that sun-bathing has been outlawed by Jack. By this time I'm into my sixth or seventh thriller. I can't remember the last time I read so many books. By 10pm that evening all but a small group in a card school had hit the sack to get a good night's rest.

The following morning we caught the coach down to the training ground for our last session there. The next day, Friday, we would have a session in the Olympic stadium on the eve of the match. It was all very laid back – if you feel any little niggle you don't train, if you are feeling knackered you don't train, if you've had a bad night's sleep and you don't want to train, don't train, if you have got a pimple on your face and you don't want to train, don't train. It's all about playing in the match against Italy and if you're just not feeling right – stay off the practice pitch. Quite a few of the team were injured. Some had suffered niggly knocks all through the competition. Paul McGrath had to rest his knee occasionally and ice it. Chris Morris had problems with his ankle. Kevin Sheedy had problems with his hamstring. At some time or another most of us, certainly the older players shall we say, especially the ones that were playing, had a little knock. Chris and Ray Houghton, people like that who did have injuries, did wonderfully well to get through the competition and play as well as they did.

As usual those who aren't playing in the five-a-sides sit and heckle the rest of us. They normally wind everybody up to fever pitch, so the five-a-sides are given an edge. But now the tackles that are going in don't carry the usual venom because of the Italian match. Afterwards we have the vote as usual – and my roommate Frank Stapleton wins the damned shirt. I think there was a conspiracy actually, because Frank is normally a good trainer, but he was given the vote. It was almost a unanimous decision.

Now Jack is slowly beginning to prepare us mentally and physically for the big match. 'Definitely no sitting out in the sun,' he warns again. 'If I catch you, you're in trouble.' The lads who wouldn't be playing against Italy, or felt that they wouldn't even be on the bench, were sneaking little sunbathing sessions all along the way. Some of these would say they were going up for a snooze. But as soon as they got in to their room the window was flung open and they took their 'snooze' lying on the floor with the rays of the sun streaking down on their lilywhite torsos! We all felt sorry for those who hadn't been involved in the games, people like Frank, Bernie Slaven, Chris Hughton, John Byrne and David Kelly. It was hard for them, but they did very well to keep their spirits up. Bernie Slaven was still doing his tourist bit that day. There was a little terrace in the hotel with a fountain and Bernie asked one of the staff to take a photograph of him and some of the others in front of the fountain. Stupid, very stupid move, but then Bernie was still finding his feet in the squad. 'Sure we'll have our picture taken with you, Bernie,' I said as I walked over to Bernie with a bunch of the lads. He was so innocent – and very wet a couple of seconds later as he hauled himself out of the fountain!

There was one big temptation in the hotel. Guinness had flown out some barrels and glasses and a small bar was set up to dispense the stuff. Cold draught Guinness – but we couldn't get our hands on it until after the match. And every time we came back into the hotel the press and local police just sat there guzzling the stuff. We could only pray that there would be some left on Saturday night.

I felt tired, probably a little nervous too, and I went to bed early that night. I had left most of the others downstairs at about 9.30-10pm. About an hour later I was awoken by someone laughing and joking and by doors opening and closing along the corridor. It wasn't until the next morning that I learned that the lads had a party – and Jack had given it the okay! He could see the agony the lads were going through watching the press downing the Guinness. 'Okay, you can have a couple,' the Big Man told them. There was a rush to the bar and I'm sure two turned into four because they ended up having a sing-song. There were antics too. Craig Johnston, the former Liverpool player who quit the game and went back to Australia, was there videoing the whole episode for a special charity film he was putting together.

TRAINING AT THE STADIO OLIMPICO

On Friday we travelled to the stadium. It's in a beautiful setting in the foothills in the northwest of the capital. The Stadio Olimpico stands at the bottom of Monte Marino and is very impressive from the outside. Built almost four decades ago, the stadium had been modernised for the World Cup finals and now was the perfect mix of old and new. All of the World Cup venues we had played in were impressive, but this was something special.

We drove into a tunnel underneath the stadium, got off the coach and into the dressingroom. When we walked out onto the pitch all we could do was marvel at the place. The playing surface was like a bowling green and the interior of the stadium was just incredible. I was feeling a little out of sorts so I just stood and watched the others train. Kevin Moran and myself spent the time just walking around, staying in the shade. It was well into the nineties again and although those who were training played the full length of the pitch, it was almost at walking pace. The session was just to keep the body ticking over. I think we were also a little superstitious and felt that we might do something before the game. Yet nobody seemed nervous. We were really looking forward to coming back to this beautiful stadium the following evening to play the Italians in their own backyard.

The session lasted just an hour and now Jack was shouting at everyone: 'Right, that's it. Don't stand in the bloody sun. Don't conduct interviews in the sun, standing there with the burning sun on your head sapping your strength.' So any interviews that needed to be done were done in the shade, in the tunnel. So long as you were out of the sun it was OK.

Back at the hotel and there were more video nasties to watch – our previous matches in the competition. We just sat there, taking the mickey out of everybody who got caught doing something funny during the games. I got the bird for shouting or kicking somebody, another lad would then be the victim for a bad tackle or a bad miss. Nobody likes watching these games but it helped kill a few hours and the boredom. Good fun. Nobody had to be told to take an early night. We all went up to try and get a good night's sleep but it was difficult. The air conditioning was not great so we left the windows open and then that let in the noise, a real Catch-22 situation. But all the lads overcome these problems. A lot of teams would not cope with them. We just had a little moan, a laugh: We're not happy with all this, but we just get on with it.

I had a telephone call from a little pal of mine in Dublin – called Mick McCarthy. Little Mick is twelve and suffers from leukaemia. He just telephoned to wish me the best for the game. Mick's call put things into perspective for me that night. How could I worry too much about a football match when little Mick was back there in Dublin fighting leukaemia?

THE MATCH AGAINST ITALY

SATURDAY, JUNE 30, THE MORNING OF THE GAME. I went into breakfast. I just couldn't stay in my bed. I'm in a room on my own now and I don't like my own company too much. After breakfast I telephone my mate Woody in England. Woody had come out to Italy with Fiona to watch a few games but when he went back home he had been admitted to hospital, so I just telephoned to see how he was. I spoke to him and that took a little weight off my mind. Little Mick had prodded my conscience to do that. After all, he was the patient telephoning me from Dublin to see how I was! After talking to Woody I telephoned Fiona in her hotel across the city. Then I phoned the kids up and spoke to them. I can't explain why I made the calls just then. Maybe you want somebody to talk to, somebody that is not involved in the game, to get away from it all completely for a few minutes. The time slipped by and we all met for lunch down in the restaurant. After that it was back up to our rooms for a snooze and later we were going to have a chat about the Italians.

The previous evening Jack was at it again. He wanted us to watch a video of the Italians. If I had actually gone and watched Schillaci and the Italian crew playing and started talking about their strong points, it wouldn't really worry me, but I didn't want to go and watch them and build them up to be something that is above and beyond me. I'm not interested basically. I will just go out and play. That might seem a bit unprofessional. It's not. I had watched the free kicks and corners, where they would put them and we had discussed who we were going to mark and all that. I didn't really want to sit and watch them in general play. I think you do watch them, then when you play them you look for something to happen that inevitably never does.

We were all back down at around 4.30pm for some tea and toast. Jack is talking to us now about the game – but never about the way the Italians play, more about what we have to do. At around 5pm we are on the coach and off to the stadium. The tape is on: 'Molly Malone', 'Red Rose Cafe', 'A Nation Once Again', 'Sean South'.

Everybody is singing, belting out the songs, getting geed up and feeling oh so proud to be on that bloody bus with the rest of the lads heading off to face the Italians. Nearing the stadium 'We Are The Boys In Green' is on and all the lads are giving it a real belting. The streets are lined with people, they have all come out, knowing we are going that way. They are all waving at us, and giving us the V sign – not the V sign as in two fingers up-you but the opposite way around like victory for them. But they were being pleasant about it, and there were no real nasty gestures. They were all waving and there was a great atmosphere. I don't think they thought there was any danger that we could win. That made us even more determined that we were going to win or at the very least give a good account of ourselves.

The crowds are lining the streets all the way, waving us in. When we get to the ground 'Sean South' is on the tape and all the lads are wound up, ready to go. There's a great feeling on the bus. We know we're going to do well, we're not worried, we have nothing to lose, we have never been such underdogs, but we're not just going to the stadium to make up the numbers. You can sense the determination – there's no way Italy are going to walk all over us. The final strains of 'Sean South' are playing as we drive down the tunnel into the stadium.

From the dressingroom to the pitch was like a morning's hike. We seemed to have to walk right under the stadium to get to the tunnel that took us out onto the pitch. We dropped our kit in the dressingroom and headed out. When we came out of the tunnel there were already quite a few fans in the stadium – many of them Irish, cheering and singing. Argentina and Yugoslavia were playing their afternoon quarter-final match in Florence and the game was being shown on the big screens in the stadium so we just sat right down on the pitch to watch it for a while as it headed towards penalties. It was good crack and John Aldridge was knocking out the jokes which helped kill any tension that might have been building up.

Then the Italian squad sort of breezed out of the tunnel. You could see the arrogance, the way they strutted out and the way they looked at us. But you could tell too that they were nervous. We knew they didn't fancy playing us – nobody would have fancied playing us. That's not being conceited. It's just the way we play and the way every time we play it's always a physically hard game against us with our never-say-die attitude. The Italians knew it was going to be a very physical challenge to beat us. After about five minutes of milling around they then decided to sit down and watch the game as well. So here we are, the two sets of players, the two teams, laid on the pitch watching Argentina defeat Yugoslavia on penalties. Then we went back into the dressingrom to prepare for the game. We had certainly won the pre-match psychological battle with the Italians.

Even though these were the quarter-finals of the World Cup, nothing had really changed. Everybody went through their own little preparations, same boring, mundane things. You don't change your routines now. The only time you change your routine is when something is going wrong. But things are going well so the routine is the same. I go for a shower, Big Tony Cascarino is coming out and John Aldridge is having a shower too. Muscles are getting rubbed down. I have a rub down under a hot shower and then slip into a cold one to cool down and to get the nerve ends tingling – liven you up, ready for the game. Some of the lads are getting strappings put on, cleaning boots – just doing the things that we always do.

We went out on the pitch for a warm-up – it didn't take long because it was still in the eighties although we were into the evening by now. We were only out on the pitch about five minutes when Jack came out patrolling and dragged us all in so we didn't tire ourselves out or use up too much energy.

Back into the dressingroom we continued with our own personal build-up. Some sat quietly, contemplating the game to come. Others walked around, cracking on, laughing and joking which is usually a nervous sign. Then Jack said he wanted a word with us and got us all to sit down.

JACK'S FINAL WORD

I will always remember the theme of his chat that evening. Nerves shouldn't come into it now, he said. We have done everything, we have come further than anybody ever anticipated. Whatever we do, nobody can criticise us now, but we want to give a good account of ourselves. Jack was very positive. 'We can win this game,' he said. 'The way we've played, if we continue the same way that we played against Romania and Holland we can beat the Italians. They're not invincible by any manner or means – even in their own their manor, on their own pitch, we can beat them.'

Jack is right because we don't have any respect for anybody when we are playing against them. Jack continued: This was the pinnacle of a footballer's career, to get to the World Cup final – and we were two games from it. Ridiculous as it might seem, Jack was right. We were just two matches from playing in the final and WE could do it.

Jack had played in one and he said it was the best thing that could happen to a footballer. To freeze now and not do the business, or certainly not to give a good account of ourselves would leave us all devastated. Jack fully believed we could win and that if we all had the same belief, then we could do it. We could go through to the semi-finals to meet Argentina. We were dead confident that if we beat Italy, we would get to the final. That's the way we were looking at it.

By now Jack had us all fired up. He told us not to expect anything from the referee. 'Italy in Rome, you are not going to get anything. If you don't get it, don't be upset about it. You should know already you're not going to get it, but go out and give a good account of yourselves and we will get a good result.'

PSYCHOLOGICAL WARFARE

So, ten minutes before the game, we're all ready, all fighting fit, pads on, rings off, taped-up, chains off, whatever you do. Then, it's out of the dressingroom. The Italian team are waiting for us to take the long walk out together. They're jumping about, there's heavy breathing and blowing and stretching and jumping and messing with their hair and their boots – all signs of nerves. They were doing little things that a fellow pro knows spell nervousness. I turned to the others and said: 'Look at them, they're not too happy at all. They're very nervous, not looking forward to what they're going to get out there. Let's go and do them.'

All the way out onto the pitch the Italians are shouting. We don't know what they're saying, but we're shouting too: 'Let's get wired into them. Win the first tackle, win the first header, win the ball, play it, chase them, close them down.' It's just a psychological thing – you shout and hopefully you intimidate the opposition. They're trying to do it to us. But our lads are just so relaxed you'd think they were smoking something!

Just before we went out onto the pitch there was a battery of television cameras. I can remember how nervous the Italians were. I had said all along that it must be terrible for them. The pressure they were under was far more intense than any other team. They were expected to win the Cup, they were the favourites playing in Rome, their home patch, in front of Europe's most fanatical fans.

Anytime we got any feedback from an interview by the Italians, they said they were going to beat us. There was no question about it, they were not worried. But now we saw the truth, the truth of it was they were having eggs. The fact was that they knew we *could* beat them. What made it even worse was the fact that they had mouthed off about it, and the press there had put us down as no-hopers. The Italian team knew different and it dawned on them that they were going out there onto the pitch for a real fight. Feelings were running very high.

Then the referee called us out onto the pitch. The noise was unbelievable. It was like a roar. All that week the stadium had been compared to the old Roman stadiums where the Christians went to die. The roar, at that moment, reminded me of all those media stories – so the roar was the lion's roar and this was his den! Then, at that moment, it was the Italians who were going to the slaughter – or at least that's the way they looked.

Our fans could hardly be seen – but we could hear them. Still, the main thing that could be made out clearly was this continuous chant of 'Italia, Italia'. Our fans could be heard, of course, when it came to the national anthem. They sang it, as usual, with a lot of pride and passion. I lost the toss again. There was no wind, no sun, no rain. Perfect conditions.

KICK-OFF

Kick-off is just minutes away. I went around the players to gee them up. I told Chris Morris to get his tackles in; Steve Staunton – don't knock any square balls up the line, be first to your challenge; Packie – come and help us, talk to us; my mate Kevin Moran – all the best, Kev, stick together, one drop off, one attack the ball; Ray Houghton – be busy, get in there. I just went through everybody. Paul McGrath – sit in front, if I get dragged out, come in behind me; Andy Townsend – get up and down, Andy, plenty of talking, help the other lads, encourage Kevin Sheedy to get forward, get his crosses in, get in the box, get on to the two lads in front of you, get them working, get Aldo to do it get Big Quinner to do it. Usual thing, just basically geeing each other up, shaking hands – we were really into it.

We started well and probably had the better of the early exchanges.

I was marking their Marty Feldman lookalike, Toto Schillaci. I had really enjoyed watching him in the competition, and I was so wound up now to play against him. I felt great, and I didn't think he was going to cause us too many problems. I was confident playing against him.

THE REFEREE

We knew we were never going to get anything from Carlos Silve Valente of Portugal. He started and he gave us nothing. Any split decision, I would have to say, he gave to the Italians. And even though we had expected that, it was still was very frustrating. Every time we challenged for the ball, he gave a free kick their way. Everytime we were in their box, he would give a free kick at the slighest challenge on anybody. It was very hard, very difficult to play in that sort of game when you were getting nothing from the officials. In fact, it came to a head in the first half. Kevin Moran applauded the referee after he finally awarded a free kick to us and he got booked for it.

I thought Kev was well out of order – the referee never deserved to be applauded at any time during the game! He stopped play at the merest suggestion of a physical challenge – not a foul, a physical challenge. He was giving all kinds of kicks at the edge of our box during the first forty-five minutes and that worried us because the Italians are very good from dead ball situations.

SCHILLACI GOAL

It came to a head just before half-time. We had done very well and then, coming from a free kick, little Schillaci pops up to finish a fine move and put the Italians in front. It was a great finish. The shot had come in, Packie parried it. The ball spun away from him, and Schillaci, from not the best of angles, ran onto it, picked his spot perfectly and shot home.

I had had a running battle with Schillaci all during the first forty-five minutes. He'd actually started it. He ran across me and was tugging at my shirt and pulling it, trying to get by me. I just held my ground, stood in his way and blocked him with my arm. So he had a dig at me. He swung his elbow and hit me in the stomach, catching me a couple of times. Of course I had a swing back, but with the difference in height he hit me in the stomach, I hit him in the eye! We ended up on the deck and had a scrap, a little tussle. Handbags at fifty paces, all a bit childish when you look back at it, but in the heat of the moment it's done. But there are no grudges held at all.

McCARTHY TEMPER

The goal came just before half-time and we were so disappointed at that going in. I remember bouncing off the park at half-time and having a go at the FIFA officials. I told them what I thought of the referee. It came as a relief. I had been dying to give him some stick, but I knew if I had I would have been booked at least, or sent off. So I kept my mouth shut and took it out on the officials.

I stormed up the tunnel, sort of kicking and stamping my feet and ended up having a run-in with Big Jack in the tunnel because I had been screaming at the two officials. He wasn't happy with that. Quite right as well I was out of order. At the time I thought I was justified, I was so annoyed and upset about the way things had gone. Not the way we played, or the fact that we were coming in 1-0 down having done so well, but decisions not going our way in the game. I wanted to win so much. I snapped back at Jack. He just laughed at me, he always laughs at me when I get on my horse anyway, thinks it hilarious when I get angry and start screaming and shouting at people. That was it. I bounced all the way up to the dressingroom, gave the guy on the door a bollicking because the door wasn't open – and it was nothing to do with him. It was just me venting my anger and frustrations on other people. When I look back at it now, I know I shouldn't have done it.

In the dressingroom, we cooled down, but we were all very frustrated at the way things were going. I was the one venting my feelings but I think everyone felt much the same way.

JACK CALMS US DOWN

Then Jack came in. Obviously he had a job to do, he had to try to calm us down. If we went out feeling like that, feeling so angry and frustrated – that's when mistakes are made. He calmed us down and told us not to lose the head. We can't just go around taking it out on the Italians, getting physical. It's only going to get worse, and if we shout and scream at the referee he is only going to get worse, if that was possible.

Jack did a good job of calming us down, told us how well we'd played, that he was very pleased with the way things had gone, and how unlucky we were. He was very pleased at the way we had created chances and basically said if we carried on like that we would get a result out of it. The Italians were not comfortable, you could see the relief on their faces when they scored. They still weren't happy, they still weren't comfortable with a 1-0 lead. So the theme was: Go out and play the very same way, try and keep control of your feelings in a very emotionally charged atmosphere.

He told us to look after each other on the park and keep playing the same way and things would happen for us, those things would come if we got a little bit of luck, a little bit of joy out of any situations that we might make. We've got a chance of getting a goal and maybe making it go to penalties, and we all know anything can happen in that situation. Had we scored, we would have put them under so much pressure. Even more pressure than they were under when they walked out for the game as the home team.

It was calm-down time, head under the cold shower, plenty of water, we were all very dehydrated. Change of shirt. Put a dry shirt on and back into the fray. We really couldn't wait to get back into it, the lads were clawing at the door to get out! Jack was trying to curb those feelings. He wanted us to be keen to win – but not over-keen, not to go out there and attack them like head cases and give something away. So he did his job well at half-time, calmed us down. We were in the right frame of mind again when we went back out into the game.

SECOND HALF

Back out into the park, back out into the cauldron, ready for the off in the second half. We kept our heads and went at them. We closed them down, created chances. We were unsettling them. The referee, however, still wasn't giving us anything. To this day I don't know how I kept my temper for the second half of that game. I am very emotional on the pitch, I want to win so badly. But this referee was giving free kicks against us all over the shop and especially against me because Schillaci and myself were having a right old battle. By now I was almost jumping with my hands behind my back to make sure I didn't 'foul' him. But he was still giving free kicks against me.

We weren't getting anywhere and time was running out. Everybody was sent upfield. The ball was pumped into their area and we hoped we'd get the equaliser by putting them under so much pressure that they would make a mistake. We threw caution to the wind. We might as well get beaten by two or three in an attempt to claw that solo goal back. It was in one of these attacks that the referee finally blew. The Italians threw their arms around each other. They were obviously delighted – and so relieved.

DISAPPOINTMENT

It was an unbelievable disappointment for us. We had said the previous evening that if we were beaten we couldn't criticise ourselves too much, we wouldn't be too disappointed. But the initial reaction to the whistle and having been knocked out of the World Cup was disbelief and disappointment. I was devastated. I picked Baresi up, shook hands with him and we agreed to exchange shirts. It sort of hit me then. I said to the lads, 'Come on, let's go and applaud the supporters,' and we all went to the middle of the field and applauded our wonderful fans who had supported us throughout all the competition so well, and who had been so well behaved. They were a credit to Ireland, a credit to us, and we wanted to show our appreciation. We applauded them and then it hit me like a bolt from above and I couldn't wait to get off the pitch. I was so disappointed. I scarpered off as quickly as I possibly could. I was in tears. I couldn't wait to get off and get into the dressingroom.

It was an incredible feeling – I just couldn't wait to get away. We had played so well and could look back on it and be very happy with a great performance, all the team. But at the time you don't think about that. We'd lost and I just wanted to get out of the park. So it was into the tunnel and I was almost marching up the bloody thing. I just wanted to get to the dressingroom and cool off, have a drink, just be alone really for a couple of minutes and try and calm down.

Baresi followed me off the pitch and shouted up the tunnel, 'Hey McCarthy,' and that helped me calm down. I went back and shook hands with him again and said, 'Well played.' I was pleased he came after me and swopped shirts because I admire the guy so much it really is a pleasure to have one of his shirts. We often talk about kids wanting our shirts and wanting players' autographs and we don't realise how much it means to them, it's only when we get a shirt from somebody we admire personally that we can actually realise what our autographs mean to the kids.

My feelings as I entered the dressingroom were in total confusion. I was angry, frustrated and disappointed. It was a different feeling to half-time. Then we had still got another half to play, the adrenalin was running high. Now I just sat down, had a drink, had a good old curse to myself and waited for the rest of the lads to come in.

Jack congratulated us on a great tournament. We had had a great time and had some success. The fact that we qualified for the quarter finals and lost to the home nation was no disgrace. He thanked us all for the way we had played and the way we had conducted ourselves. He said: 'I know you are disappointed, but don't be too disappointed. Everybody who has been here – not just the players – has distinguished himself as a part of the Irish squad.' Then we got called – they asked me to go on television. You can imagine how I felt when they came in and asked Jack and myself to go on television. I couldn't wait to get there. I was going to get on and I was going to give this referee some stick. I have Big Jack to thank for a lot of things, but especially for this – just as we were sitting down in the RTE studio in front of the TV cameras he said to me: 'Don't criticise the ref, don't let anybody see that you are that upset, sour grapes, that's all people will think it is.' I realised he was right. If I had criticised the referee I would get myself into trouble for bringing the game into disrepute.

Later I thought: The referee is out there to do a job and he did it. We might not agree with everything he did, but anyway it's over now and we can only look back on it with a bit of pride. The fact was we had enjoyed ourselves and it had been a privilege and a pleasure to be out there. It was hard to say my few words for the TV.

When I got back to the dressingroom it had been invaded by the Italian players. It was major swop time. Shirts, tracksuits, tee-shirts – the lot. They weren't a bad bunch after all. It was a nice atmosphere. We had been deadly enemies on the field, but now we were just fellow professionals and friends.

I had a shower. Frank was in there and we went over the game again. I was beginning to come down from it. The fans were still outside, chanting our names. We all wanted to go out and see them again, but the stadium security refused to let us out. A beer and back on the bus.

The tapes are on again on the way back to the hotel and the sing-song starts. But there was a little job I had to do. As we came out of the stadium a reporter told me that Kevin Moran was thinking of retiring. I walked down the bus and put my case to him. We had got on well together, had been through a lot together and had had a lot of respect for each other. It might not have been the time or the place to do it, but I knew I had to let him know how I felt. I didn't want Kevin to step down from the squad. The rest of the lads were going around patting each other on the back and telling each other how well we had done. We were all looking forward to getting back to the hotel to see our wives – and to knock back the Guinness!

The Guinness was there, ready and waiting, when we got back to the hotel – and so were our wives. It was going to be a good night, our last in Italy after twenty-two days that none of the lads will ever forget. We were going to let ourselves go and enjoy the fact that we had done so well – and forget the game for a few hours. Although a little disappointed still about the result, I was also a little relieved it was all over. Soon I would be going home to see my kids and get some semblance of order back in my life. We went straight in to eat when we arrived at the hotel. Well, straight in after a couple of pints of Guinness. There were just the players, their wives, some relatives and close friends there, and the atmosphere was wonderful.

There was still, obviously, talk about the game. But we were talking about other things – what the kids had been up to, how much they had grown, what was happening at home. I had only been away for about six weeks to Dublin, Turkey, Malta and Italy, but I missed them a lot. After we had eaten, people began to drift out to the bar.

The reception area, the foyer and the verandah outside were packed. Fiona and I went and sat around the fountain in the grounds. I got a bit of abuse for moving out – we were on a lovers' trip, that kind of stuff! It was no such thing we were just too warm inside.

Gradually another couple joined us and then another. Soon everybody had come into the garden. It was a lovely night and we all sat around under the umbrellas. Then Kevin Moran did his MC bit again. He stood up on a stool and said it was about time we got a sing-song going. That was the start of a great night. We were all getting well oiled with the Guinness – and with relief that it was all over. Now we could really let go and enjoy ourselves. The sing-song started. Everybody was standing up, doing their bit. Niall Quinn sang two or three songs. He had come out of his shell, out of the woodwork, and did a couple of great turns for us.

One fairly distingushed guest was Chris De Burgh. He sang 'Lady In Red' which was terrific. Then he tried to sing two or three other songs – and he couldn't remember the words. He was the worst singer of the lot! I think he must have had more Guinness than the rest of us! But he was great. Just the fact that he was there was nice. Frank's dad, Mick Stapleton, stood up and did a song for us. Craig Johnston was there again, still making his video. He got into the fountain so he could have some room because the garden was full. By now, after a few pints of Guinness, I was beginning to get a little busy. I felt Craig couldn't be allowed in the fountain without being dunked. So some of the lads and myself picked him up and splash! He didn't mind at all. He just asked someone to take a picture of him in all his soggy glory! We sat there soaking wet, we sat and sang and sang. The night went by so quickly. People began to drift away, hoping to snatch a few hours of shut-eye. That was going to be difficult – it was almost 6am as Fiona and I headed to our room and they were still singing, and the birds were joining them in the dawn chorus. I was still wet outside from the fountain episode and was well and truly wet inside after drinking enough Guinness to last me a lifetime.

So we went and crashed out in a coma, it wasn't a sleep, it was a drunken coma. But I was up at nine o'clock, showered, shaved, and down for breakfast. I tucked in and then set the example for everybody else and put a lot of the lads under pressure – I took a tray up to Fiona. Some of the others taunted me, but a few minutes later I saw them doing the same thing. It's Sunday, there's no more training or games.

We're going home and we've been told to expect a 'good' reception when we get there. For the last time, we have to go through the boring process of packing. By this time there's so much in the cases that I'm sitting on them and Fiona is trying to lock them. There is so much stuff – presentations, mementos. You've got to take them all with you, and all that dirty washing as well. We took the cases downstairs, had a meal and then it was off on the bus to the airport. The drinking has started again – it's a hair of the dog that bit you. I made an excuse for having another Guinness. It was one for all and all for one with us – if the others were going to have a pint then I wasn't going to be left out. As the coach moved off from the hotel for the last time the staff and many of the locals came out to wave us off. Maybe they were just glad to see the back of us after giving their national team such a hard match! But it was lovely, a nice little touch. I will always have a soft spot for Italy.

THE HOMECOMING

AER LINGUS HAD SENT A PLANE OVER FOR US and we were all on it, the players, management and our wives. But we were all split up. We all wanted to be together and continue the party, the longest sing-song in history. But on the plus side was the fact that we were able to get an hour's sleep. It was, ironically, an uneventful flight. Just as well, because when the lads get going it can be pandemonium. We kept getting told we'd have an unbelievable reception waiting for us when we got to Dublin. We'd had a teriffic reception when we came back after the European championships and we thought that couldn't be bettered. But as we approach Dublin the captain tells us the place has come to a standstill. He did one or two circles over the city to prove his point. It *was* an incredible sight – people stretched from the airport all the way into the centre of the city.

When the door opened you couldn't hear a word for the noise. It was almost embarrassing, the fact that all these people were there to cheer the team. It was overwhelming. We hadn't won the World Cup – I shudder to think what would have happened if we did. Everybody wanted to shake our hands, pat us on the back, just touch. The welcome at the airport was phenomenal. I stood and looked at the place. It was so full you'd wonder would it collapse under the weight. I can't remember what Jack said, I was so stunned.

Then we were told about the open-top bus to take us into the city. But that was one trip that almost didn't happen. Having been split from our wives on the plane we were now told that they would travel on a separate bus behind ours. We were disappointed, but that was the way it was to be. Then when we got on the first bus there were loads of people there who hadn't even been to the World Cup who could easily have travelled on the second bus. I was a little annoyed to say the least. Fiona had come out to Sardinia, got chucked in a tip of a hotel 300 kilometres away from me, lost her car in Palermo and had to leave a tip of a hotel in Rome. But she had been at all the matches, and I felt she and the rest of the wives and girlfriends who had gone through so much should be with us. After a few 'diplomatic' words with the powers that be, they were allowed on our bus.

I have never ever seen so many people cram the streets of any city in my life. It was incredible all the way into the centre. It was dangerous at times when you saw young kids getting so close to the wheels – and it was still embarrassing for us, this incredible turnout. But then we got into it. We couldn't do enough for them. We were trying to wave at everyone. If you caught somebody's eye and waved at them their face lit up, and you knew you had made their day. It was a terrific feeling, the fact that you could actually have that effect on somebody. The trip in was brilliant. The little thing of being split up on the plane and not being able to sit with each other and the fact that we had to battle a little bit to get the wives on the bus was just history by now. The fans had waited so long that day to welcome us home and there they were, singing all the songs. If the bus stopped the crowd would burst into 'Molly Malone'. We began to join in. Paul McGrath is not that happy about 'Ooh Aah, Paul McGrath' – but now the team were singing it too!

Right down the main road from the airport all the way into O'Connell Street the roads and streets were throbbing with people. If we had walked to College Green where they had planned to have a reception for us it would have taken half the time. It seemed that the whole country had hit town for the weekend to welcome us home. The players – and their wives – were totally overwhelmed. We just couldn't believe it. There was a few tears on the bus – and not just from our wives!

But Big Jack, the centre of attention as usual, was uneasy. He was diving up and down the bus. 'Get him, watch him, he's falling under the wheel, don't let him go, watch him. Get that bloody kid out of there,' he was screaming. He was agitated and genuinely worried about the kids.

O'Connell Street was something else, from there right over to College Green the bus crawled along and the noise, the deafening noise, the songs, the chants continued. We were real heroes to these people. It made us all feel somewhat humble. It took us almost thirty minutes to get from the beginning of College Green into the Bank of Ireland – a journey of less than a hundred yards. I thought we would never get there – I was dying to get to a toilet! We had been on the bus for over four hours.

Then we went out to the front of the bank where they had erected a podium. It was great, we could really share the homecoming with all those wonderful people in the Green. When all the players were on the podium I was asked, as captain, to introduce them. But Big Jack stole the show. He began to do the business and gave a little speech about each individual player. I made my speech totally off the cuff. I thanked everybody, the people who had travelled, the people at home who had given us such wonderful support, for a great homecoming, just thanked everybody on behalf of us all. We were all presented to the supporters who gave each and every one of us a wonderful reception.

When everybody had been presented it was our turn to sing! We sang 'Molly Malone' and some of the officials were trying to drag us off to go into the bank and meet everybody in there, but the lads were enjoying it. It was a terrific day. We were all knackered at the end, but it was so memorable.

Inside the bank it was sausages on sticks, vol-au-vents, bits of chicken, little hot savouries, another interview for television and a pint if you could drink one. And you were signing autographs or having your picture taken, looking this way, turning the other way ...

We had had a long day, it was getting very, very tiring and even when that was finished we couldn't get on the bus. The fans wouldn't let us out the gate. Eventually we rounded everybody up, that was the hard part, but we managed. We got onto the coach and home. It was getting late and we were all looking forward to a couple of quiet jars in the bar back at the hotel. But the hotel was bedlam too. It was packed. I can appreciate the way people felt, everybody wanted to pat me on the back or shake my hand, which is lovely, but when they all want to do it at once it is all a bit too much. It gradually wore me down. I was wrecked and decided to call it a day.

On Monday afternoon I went home, just dying to see the kids. I was also feeling a little depressed, coming to terms with what had happened. But that would take another day or two. Fiona and I arrived home late on Tuesday evening. The girls, Katie and Anna, were up waiting for me. It was lovely, I so much wanted to see them. I wanted to see the little fella, Michael, too. But he was upstairs in bed. I just went up and gave him a cuddle while he slept. I was going to get him up but that was for purely selfish reasons, and like his dad he'd have been ratty the next day! The next morning he just came into our bedroom, got into the bed and fell asleep. It was great to see he hadn't changed too much in the five weeks I had been away.

Now I could look back and reflect on what had happened to me over those glorious weeks. I probably enjoyed it more now, reflecting on it, than I did when I was there. Memories? There are millions of them. Highlights? The same. I was so proud to be part of it all, leading my country out in their first ever World Cup finals; the sheer exhilaration of playing in the finals – Cagliari, Palermo, Genoa, Rome, meeting the Pope, the homecoming; the fans, those wonderful fans. Now I was back with my family, home to rest and to spend some time with them. And there were no more training camps and living with twenty-one other blokes. And no more yellow jerseys. But I loved every minute of it. When are we going again, Jack?

JACK CHARLTON

WHEN JACK TOOK OVER AS MANAGER of the Irish team I had already known him for quite a while. He and I shared the same local just outside Barnsley when he was manager at Sheffield Wednesday and I was still at Barnsley Football Club. He'd come and have a pint and sometimes a game with the locals.

Jack's first Ireland game was against Wales in March 1986. He picked his squad – and I was out! My old drinking mate had dropped me. Somebody asked him about me and he said: 'I don't need to pick Mick McCarthy, I know what he's like.' That wasn't much consolation to me at the time. I wanted to be part of things. I thought, This is it, I'm finished at international level. But then I had always hoped for maybe a dozen caps and I had eleven so I hadn't done too badly. Then he phoned me – and I had just come back from the PFA Dinner and I was a little high – but I sobered up quick enough and was on the plane to Dublin the following morning. Jack brought me on in the second-half against Wales on March 26, 1986. We were beaten 1-0 by an Ian Rush goal and their 'keeper Neville Southall broke his ankle when he fell awkwardly on the Lansdowne Road surface. Jack came in for a bit of stick after that game from those who thought he should never have been given the job. But that criticism only made him more determined to do well.

By the time we played Uruguay the following month, Jack was beginning to formulate his plan of action. Our attempts to play European-style football were thrown out the window. 'You can cut that out for a start,' Jack said. 'You all play in the English or Scottish League so we will play British-style football and let the other team bloody well try and come to grips with it.' We drew 1-1 with Uruguay and Jack's ideas were beginning to take shape. Jack's style suited me down to the ground. The way he wanted us to play meant that I got a chance to do what I do best – playing centre-half, getting close to a striker and doing a job of stopping him scoring.

The turning point for Republic of Ireland soccer came in April 1986. Jack took the team to Iceland for an international tournament. It gave him a chance, over a period of five or six days, to assess the players and to start building team spirit.

Jack also showed the lads his lighter side as we flew into Reykjavik for the tournament. At the time Iceland had peculiar licensing laws. You could drink things like whiskey and vodka until it came out your ears, but there was a total ban on beer. You couldn't get it for love nor money in the place. So as we were coming off the plane Jack told the lads to stock up on the beer at the Duty Free Shop. Through customs and the press were waiting for us – twenty-two players and officials all carrying a carry-out containing twenty-four beers tucked under their arms! I don't think any other manager in the world would have allowed it. Here we were, living up to what many of them thought about the Irish! Jack worked on us, getting his ideas across and on May 25 we played the home nation and beat them 2-1.

CAPTAIN

Two days later we met Czechoslovakia in the final of the tournament and won that with a Frank Stapleton goal. We had won TWO games on foreign soil. For that final Jack had made me captain, so the first time the Republic won anything at senior level I was captain. That meant a lot to me.

The whole squad got on well together. That trip to Iceland was where the team spirit began to come together. Jack worked on it and kept drumming into us how he wanted us to play. He was also getting to know the players and they were reacting to him as well. I was lucky in that I had known him before, I knew about his sense of humour and I also knew that underneath that stern and abrasive exterior was a kind and caring man who was full of fun and wit. I remember back in Barnsley when he walked into the pub one night. I was with a group of friends and their wives and girlfriends. I went to the bar. 'Will you have a drink, Jack?' I asked. The big man said he wanted a pint so I got him one. A little later I was at the bar again and he asked me if I wanted a drink and I told him No, I was getting a round. 'No, I'll get it,' he said. 'Are you sure?' I inquired. 'Of course, what is it?' So I told him, two pints of lager, a pint of bitter, a vodka and lime and two fruit juices. He brought them over to the table. Then he bent over and whispered in my ear: 'Mick, don't ever buy me a pint again!' I broke up laughing – I'd caught him accidentally, but he would never let it happen again.

Just two short years after that initial success in Iceland, Jack took us to the European Championships. And two years on we were at the World Cup finals. In the space of just four-and-a-half years the man has taken Irish soccer from being the laughing stock of Europe to a place in the top ten nations in the world. I don't think anybody else could have done it. He's done it his way and has earned the respect and thanks of almost everybody in the country. He's also earned the respect of every player he has come in contact with at international level.

HANDLING THE PLAYERS

He has his own peculiar way of handling the players – but it works. He gave Tony Cascarino a terrible time when he first came into one of his squads. Jack would mooch up behind Cas when he was playing cards with some of the lads, sit looking over his shoulder and say, 'Okay, I'm playing now.' Cas would say, 'No, you're not, I was in here first.' Then Jack would just turn and look at him and say, 'Well, I won't pick you again.' Cas wouldn't know if he was being serious or not. The rest of the lads would know it was a wind-up, but Cas would move over and let Jack play. Other times he would just sit on Tony's shoulder and say, 'Why did you play that?' and he'd just ruin any chance he had of winning that particular hand.

JACK CHARLTON DON'TS!

Never place a bet with Jack. If he wins he collects, if he loses he'll just say that he was only joking when he placed the bet – that's why I haven't paid him the £10 I owe him from the European Championships!

Never give Jack money for the phone. Once, on the way back from a trip abroad, we landed in Manchester. Jack had no change and he asked me for ten pence for the phone. I took some change out of my pocket and he picked out a fifty pence piece. A local call was ten pence. If that had been Jack's brass he would have gone looking for change of the fifty pence!

Then there's all these fishing trips he goes on down the country.

He'd ask at a pub or local shop would they cash a cheque for him. Of course they will. But they never cash them – the cheques are mounted and put up on the wall! So Jack has written all these cheques which have never been cashed. He's delighted. I've warned Jack though, one day when it changes those cheques will be heading into local banks all over the country and his balance will take a bit of a hammering.

What you see is what you get. That's Jack. Nothing is for show. I think you have to admire him for that. He's wonderfully single-minded, he's got his opinions and ideas on how the game should be played. Jack is very knowledgeable on the game. He'll go and watch a game, then he's got this picture of it, and he can remember everything that happened. If it's relevant to what he wants to talk about he'll remember it. He will scribble a load of notes, he'll read them and then he'll say: 'I haven't got my glasses, I can't remember what I wrote there. Anyway, it doesn't matter and to hell with the notes.' But he can forget your name – he called Paul McGrath John McGrath and he called Pat Byrne Mick Byrne for a month. He writes names down too, but if he can't remember our lads' names what chance has he got with the likes of Ivan Kusnetsov or Zbigniew Boniek? Jack doesn't worry about the peripheral things. He simplifies everything – the way we play, the way we eat. He gives the lads a lot of freedom. Jack is a realist and he knows when he's had enough of the players and when they've had enough of him. When the time comes that the FAI or the fans become disaffected with him, he will jump the gun – he will go before they ask him to. He chooses his moments perfectly. The job as Irish manager is not the be-all and end-all for Jack. Maybe that's why he has been so successful. When Jack arrived as manager some of the lads were a little sceptical to say the least. Then when he started talking about the game he made everything simple. He uses one word instead of ten. If he thinks you are a dumbo, he says so.

But Jack is a mug when it comes to kids – he loves them. Coming back from the World Cup the homecoming was ruined for him because he was really worried some youngster would get injured in the crowds or fall under our bus.

Another time, after we trained at Dalymount Park one afternoon, we're all getting back onto the coach and the kids are all milling around him beside a busy road and he's roaring at them: 'Watch that car, get off the road, move in.'

Then when he got on the bus he turned around to us and just said: 'Does anybody fancy an ice cream?' All the lads screamed, 'I do.' So Jack is back off the bus, across the busy road with all these kids in tow, walks into a shop and orders twenty-six ice creams! That's Jack for you.

My strongest memory of Jack came immediately after our civic reception when we returned from the European Championships. Back at our hotel, Packie and I had planned to go out for a Chinese meal with our wives. We had washed, showered and got dressed up and we were just coming out of our room when Jack walked up to me and asked what was happening. I told him and he asked me could his wife and himself tag along. 'Of course,' I said. He's great crack to be with. When we got to the restaurant the word soon got around that we had arrived. The place was already jammed and now the word had spread to the street outside.

Then Jack decides he's going to treat us and pick up the bill. I was made up – this was something I could go back and tell the rest of the lads and they wouldn't believe it! Then Jack starts: 'Right, what are we going to have?' And before you can open your mouth, Jack is ordering for all of us. He takes over the place wherever he is. He gets a menu. 'Shall we share and pick at each?' Then he's really off: 'I'll have that – you have that, you have that.' Jack orders the six main courses and then five starters – and a crab and sweetcorn soup for himself, and he still expects to share our starters. I said: 'You cheeky beggar. Are we all getting six spoons for the soup?' Then everybody's at him. He's stitched us up. And then when he went up to pay for the meal – it's already been paid for. I'm shattered – he's got away with it again.

EAMON DUNPHY

There have been two times when I've seen Jack almost lose his temper, once just after the European Championships and the other during the World Cup. On both occasions one person was to blame – Eamon Dunphy.

When Jack walked out of this press conference at the World Cup because Dunphy was there he came in for some unfair criticism. Not many people knew the reason for his walkout – and it had more to do with an incident at the European Championships than with comments Dunphy made during the World Cup. I have talked to some of the players in the squad since and they all felt that the record had to be put straight – and Jack's reputation protected.

Eamon has upset many of the players down through the years. At first we thought that his knowledge of the game would give him a better insight into the problems that professional football players face. He also knew the set-up within the Irish squad as a former international player. Now as a journalist we all felt – well, he's one of us, he knows the problems and we could expect somebody to write intelligently without all the hype.

But Eamon's articles appeared to be personal attacks on some of the players. Before we went to Germany he had already made plenty of enemies in the squad. At the European Championships we bent over backwards to accommodate the press. We were always available to do interviews. But Jack had set one room aside for the players no matter where we were during the Championships, a room which only the players and management team had access to.

Then, just after the match against the Soviet Union, Jack walked into the room with Eamon. The atmosphere changed immediately. Frank Stapleton, my roommate, got up and walked out. I followed him, but not before I had told Eamon in no uncertain terms that I wouldn't remain in the same room as him. Jack was flabbergasted. He didn't know what was going on. When Eamon left, Liam Brady went up to Jack and the boss asked him what was going on. Liam told him that Eamon had got off lightly – he was surprised I hadn't knocked his block off! When Frank and I came back into the room Jack was fuming.

He told us he had brought Eamon into the room only because we were eating there and Eamon wanted to ask Jack some questions. Now because of all the fuss he had missed his food. Soon, however, Jack was told how the players felt about Eamon – that they felt his articles, for the most part, had been personal attacks on them. We sat up for a few drinks that evening and the whole conversation revolved around what had happened that day. By the end of the evening Jack realised how we felt and apologised to us all. I told him that I knew that after I had had my say to Eamon in front of the squad that soon afterwards Eamon would have his say about me in front of thousands of newspaper readers. I knew it would be fairly personal from now on.

And true to form on the Sunday we were travelling back from Germany it happened. We all got on the plane and Jack sat there reading a paper. He apologised to me. I could see he was furious. He told me that Eamon had had a go at me in the newspaper. 'Let's see it, Jack,' I said leaning over his seat. 'No, I don't think you should read it. It will ruin the day,' he replied. But I read it – and it did hurt – but it didn't ruin my day. It was, as I expected, a very personal attack. All Eamon left out was that maybe my father should have been excommunicated and thrown out of his native Waterford! A day or so later Eamon walked into our hotel. Jack saw him, went straight over to him and let loose with a verbal barrage. Within minutes Eamon had left. Jack came back in and we asked him what had happened: Jack had just told him that if you try to hurt one of my lads you try to hurt all of them. Jack also told him that he had tried to destroy me on what was then the greatest day in Irish soccer history as we returned from Germany. Eamon was also told that the Irish soccer team and their fans had done more for Irish tourism in one week than Bord Failte had done in a year. The boss also made it clear to Eamon that he would have nothing to do with him again. It's something that we had learned – the hard way – somewhat earlier. So that's why Jack wouldn't talk to Eamon at his World Cup press conference. He was sticking by his players.

Jack has changed a lot of our lives – players and fans. He has made us all proud to be Irish. He lifted the nation for almost a month this summer – a summer in which crime figures went down and people forgot rivalries as their nation went soccer-mad. It takes a special kind of person to do that. Jack Charlton is one of those.